PRACTICAL GUIDE TO BUILDING AN API BACK END WITH SPRING BOOT

Wim Deblauwe

Practical Guide to Building an API Back End with Spring Boot

© 2018 Wim Deblauwe. All rights reserved. Version 1.0.2.

Published by C4Media, publisher of InfoQ.com.

No part of this publication may be reproduced, stored in a retrieval system or transmitted in any form or by any means, electronic, mechanical, photocopying, recoding, scanning or otherwise except as permitted under Sections 107 or 108 of the 1976 United States Copyright Act, without the prior written permission of the publisher.

Production Editor: Ana Ciobotaru
Copy Editor: Lawrence Nyveen
Cover and Interior Design: Dragos Balasoiu

Library of Congress Cataloguing-in-Publication Data: ISBN: 978-0-359-04452-8

Table of Contents

Dedication 1
Acknowledgements 2
Preface 3
    What is in an InfoQ mini-book? 3
    Who this book is for 3
    What you need for this book 3
    Conventions 4
    Reader feedback 5
Introduction 7
What Is Spring Boot? 9
    Spring Framework 10
    Spring Boot 10
Getting Started 11
    Preparation 12
    Spring Initializr 12
    Properties 16
    Spring profiles 17
    Configure logging 19
    Source code for the book 23
CopsBoot 25
    Explanation of the sample project 26
    Generating the project skeleton 26
User Management 29
    User domain 30
    User repository 34
    User-domain refactoring 37
    Summary 45
REST API Security 47
    Spring Security OAuth2 48
    UserDetailsService 52
    Supporting beans 63
    Test getting an access token 64
    Summary 76

User REST Controller	77
Basics	78
Get mapping	78
POST mapping	87
Writing API documentation	91
Refactoring to avoid duplication	109
Summary	111
Working with a Real Database	113
Installation of PostgreSQL	114
Using PostgreSQL	115
Updates	120
Integration testing	120
Summary	125
Validation	127
Built-in validators	128
Unit test for a built-in validator	130
Handling validation errors via an exception handler	131
Custom field validator	134
Custom object validator	141
Custom object validator using a Spring service	143
Summary	147
File Upload	149
Upload a file	150
File-size validation	153
Summary	157
Action!	159
Additional reading	159
About the Author	161
Appendix A: OAuth Database Schema	163
PostgreSQL	163
MySQL	165
Microsoft SQL Server	165
H2	166

Dedication

I would like to dedicate this book to my wife Sofie and sons Victor and Jules, as I was more absent while trying to put my knowledge into this book. Their continued support for all my endeavours means the world to me.

Acknowledgements

I would also like to thank all the people that made Spring and Spring Boot a reality. It is really an amazing piece of software.

I also want to send a big thank you to the people that created Asciidoctor. It made writing this book extremely enjoyable.

Finally, I also want to thank the book's editors, Ben Evans and Lawrence Nyveen. Their feedback has been invaluable for making this book the best it can be.

Preface

This book is the culmination of two years of working with Spring Boot on a variety of projects. This is the book I wished I had when starting out building back-end applications with Java and Spring Boot.

Through the creation of a fictional application called CopsBoot, you will learn about Spring, Spring Boot, Spring Security, and Spring Data. You will also learn to use unit and integration tests to ensure the proper code functionality and build a maintainable code base that you can expand upon.

This book assumes you have enough basic Java knowledge to be able to follow. However, proficiency in similar languages like C# should be sufficient.

What is in an InfoQ mini-book?

InfoQ mini-books are designed to be concise, intending to serve technical architects looking to get a firm conceptual understanding of a new technology or technique in a quick yet in-depth fashion. You can think of these books as covering a topic strategically or essentially. After reading a mini-book, the reader should have a fundamental understanding of a technology, including when and where to apply it, how it relates to other technologies, and an overall feeling that they have assimilated the combined knowledge of other professionals who have already figured out what this technology is about. The reader will then be able to make intelligent decisions about the technology once their projects require it, and can delve into sources of more detailed information (such as larger books or tutorials) at that time.

Who this book is for

This book is for Java developers that want to quickly start creating a REST API using Spring Boot.

What you need for this book

To try code samples in this book, you will need a computer running an up-to-date operating system (Windows, Linux, or macOS). You will need Java installed. The book code was tested against JDK 8, but newer versions should also work.

Conventions

We use a number of typographical conventions within this book that distinguish between different kinds of information.

Code in the text, including commands, variables, file names, CSS class names, and property names are shown as follows:

> Spring Boot uses a `public static void main` entry point that launches an embedded web server for you.

A block of code is set out as follows. It may be coloured, depending on the format in which you're reading this book.

src/main/java/demo/DemoApplication.java

```
@RestController
class BlogController {
    private final BlogRepository repository;

    // Yay! No annotations needed for constructor injection in Spring 4.3+.
    public BlogController(BlogRepository repository) {
        this.repository = repository;
    }

    @RequestMapping("/blogs")
    Collection<Blog> list() {
        return repository.findAll();
    }
}
```

When we want to draw your attention to certain lines of code, those lines are annotated using numbers accompanied by brief descriptions.

```
@SpringBootApplication ①
public class Application {

        public static void main(String[] args) {
                SpringApplication.run(Application.class, args);
        }
}
```

① The `@SpringBootApplication` annotation marks this class as the main class when starting with Spring Boot.

 Tips are shown using callouts like this.

 Warnings are shown using callouts like this.

> **Sidebar**
>
> Additional information about a certain topic may be displayed in a sidebar like this one.

Finally, this text shows what a quote looks like:

> In the end, it's not the years in your life that count. It's the life in your years.
>
> — Abraham Lincoln

Reader feedback

We always welcome feedback from our readers. Let us know what you thought about this book — what you liked or disliked. Reader feedback helps us develop titles that deliver the most value to you.

To send us feedback, e-mail us at feedback@infoq.com [mailto:feedback@infoq.com].

If you're interested in writing a mini-book for InfoQ, see http://www.infoq.com/minibook-guidelines.

Introduction

I have been working with Spring Boot for over two years and it has made development a tremendous joy. It is important in our fast-paced world to be able to prototype quickly, but also to ensure that you are not doing any wasted work.

For me, this is one of the major strengths of Spring Boot. The smallest application can fit in a tweet [https://twitter.com/rob_winch/status/364871658483351552], yet your application will scale to Internet scale with the greatest of ease.

Combine Spring Boot with Spring Data and Spring Security and you can have something up and running in no time. And it is not just "something", it is a solid base to build upon.

CHAPTER ONE

What Is Spring Boot?

Spring Framework

Spring Boot is based upon the Spring Framework [https://projects.spring.io/spring-framework/], which is at its core a dependency-injection container. Spring makes it easy to define everything in your application as loosely coupled components which Spring will tie together at run time. Spring also has a programming model that allows you to make abstractions from specific deployment environments.

One of the key things you need to understand is that Spring is based on the concept of "beans" or "components", which are basically singletons without the drawbacks of the traditional singleton pattern [https://en.wikipedia.org/wiki/Singleton_pattern].

With dependency injection, each component just declares the collaborators it needs, and Spring provides them at run time. The biggest advantage is that you can easily inject different instances for different deployment scenarios of your application (e.g., staging versus production versus unit tests).

Spring Boot

The Spring Boot website explains itself succinctly:

> Spring Boot makes it easy to create stand-alone, production-grade Spring based Applications that you can "just run". We take an opinionated view of the Spring platform and third-party libraries so you can get started with minimum fuss. Most Spring Boot applications need very little Spring configuration.

With Spring Boot, you get up and running with your Spring application in no time, without the need to deploy to a container like Tomcat or Jetty. You can just run the application right from your IDE.

Spring Boot also ensures that you get a list of versions of libraries inside and outside of the Spring portfolio that are guaranteed to work together without problems.

CHAPTER TWO

Getting Started

Preparation

Before you can start, you need to install some things:

1. Java: Download the JDK 8 from http://www.oracle.com/technetwork/java/javase/downloads/index.html
2. Maven: Follow the instructions at https://maven.apache.org/install.html to install Maven. If you are on a UNIX-based platform, you might want to use SDKMAN! [https://sdkman.io/install] to make this easier.

Spring Initializr

The easiest way to get started with Spring Boot is to create a project using Spring Initializr. This web application allows you to generate a Spring Boot project with the option of including all the dependencies you need.

To get started, open your favorite browser at https://start.spring.io/ [https://start.spring.io/]

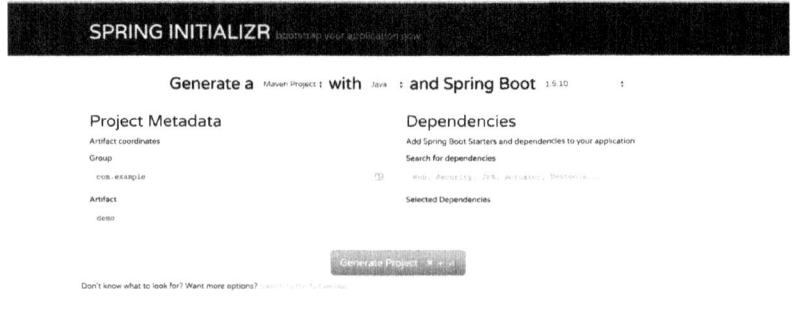

Figure 1. The Spring Initializr website.

Start with the defaults:

- Maven [https://maven.apache.org/] as build system;
- Java 8 [https://www.oracle.com/java/index.html] as programming language; and
- Spring Boot version 2.0.3, as this is the most recent version at the time of writing.

You can use Gradle as your build system or one of the other supported JVM languages if you prefer to. The main principles explained in the book remain the same.

Start out simple and only include Web and Lombok as dependencies.

 Project Lombok [https://projectlombok.org/] lets you avoid having to write boilerplate code in Java like getters, setters, equals(), hashCode(), ...

Press "Generate Project" and unzip the file to a location of your choice.

The generated project contains the following files and directories:

```
pom.xml ①
mvnw ②
mvnw.cmd
src
  |-- main
      |-- java
          |-- com.springbook.application
              |-- Application ③
      |-- resources
          |-- application.properties
  |-- test
      |-- java
          |-- com.springbook.application
              |-- ApplicationTests ④
```

① pom.xml defines the Maven configuration of the project.

② mvnw and mvnw.cmd allows the project to build even if you don't have Maven installed via the Maven Wrapper [https://github.com/takari/maven-wrapper].

③ The starting point of the application having a main() that lets you run and debug the application. from your favorite IDE without having to deploy to a container like Tomcat.

④ A unit test that starts your application to check if at least the Spring context loads properly.

Let's take a closer look at Application.java:

Application.java

```
@SpringBootApplication ①
public class Application {

    public static void main(String[] args) {
        SpringApplication.run(Application.class, args);
    }
}
```

① The `@SpringBootApplication` annotation marks this class as the main class when starting with Spring Boot.

Not much code, right? However, if you run this `main`, you will notice that a lot of things are happening under the hood.

You can run the application from your IDE or through Maven with `mvn spring-boot:run`. See Running your application [https://docs.spring.io/spring-boot/docs/current/reference/html/using-boot-running-your-application.html] in the Spring Boot documentation for more information.

```
  .   ____          _            __ _ _
 /\\ / ___'_ __ _ _(_)_ __  __ _ \ \ \ \
( ( )\___ | '_ | '_| | '_ \/ _` | \ \ \ \
 \\/  ___)| |_)| | | | | || (_| |  ) ) ) )
  '  |____| .__|_| |_|_| |_\__, | / / / /
 =========|_|==============|___/=/_/_/_/
 :: Spring Boot ::        (v2.0.3.RELEASE)

 2018-07-07 14:32:28.272  INFO 4838 --- [           main]
com.springbook.application.Application   : Starting Application on Wims-
MacBook-Pro.local with PID 4838 (started by wdb in
/Users/wdb/Projects/spring-boot-book/src/example-code/chapter02/01 -
Generated project)
 2018-07-07 14:32:28.276  INFO 4838 --- [           main]
com.springbook.application.Application   : No active profile set, falling
back to default profiles: default
 2018-07-07 14:32:28.319  INFO 4838 --- [           main]
ConfigServletWebServerApplicationContext : Refreshing
org.springframework.boot.web.servlet.context.AnnotationConfigServletWebServer
ApplicationContext@288c63fb: startup date [Sat Jul 07 14:32:28 CEST 2018];
root of context hierarchy
 2018-07-07 14:32:29.179  INFO 4838 --- [           main]
o.s.b.w.embedded.tomcat.TomcatWebServer  : Tomcat initialized with port(s):
8080 (http)
 2018-07-07 14:32:29.204  INFO 4838 --- [           main]
o.apache.catalina.core.StandardService   : Starting service [Tomcat]
 2018-07-07 14:32:29.205  INFO 4838 --- [           main]
org.apache.catalina.core.StandardEngine  : Starting Servlet Engine: Apache
```

```
Tomcat/8.5.31
 2018-07-07 14:32:29.214  INFO 4838 --- [ost-startStop-1]
o.a.catalina.core.AprLifecycleListener   : The APR based Apache Tomcat Native
library which allows optimal performance in production environments was not
found on the java.library.path:
[/Users/wdb/Library/Java/Extensions:/Library/Java/Extensions:/Network/Library
/Java/Extensions:/System/Library/Java/Extensions:/usr/lib/java:.]
 2018-07-07 14:32:29.285  INFO 4838 --- [ost-startStop-1]
o.a.c.c.C.[Tomcat].[localhost].[/]       : Initializing Spring embedded
WebApplicationContext
 2018-07-07 14:32:29.285  INFO 4838 --- [ost-startStop-1]
o.s.web.context.ContextLoader            : Root WebApplicationContext:
initialization completed in 969 ms
 2018-07-07 14:32:29.386  INFO 4838 --- [ost-startStop-1]
o.s.b.w.servlet.ServletRegistrationBean  : Servlet dispatcherServlet mapped
to [/]
 2018-07-07 14:32:29.388  INFO 4838 --- [ost-startStop-1]
o.s.b.w.servlet.FilterRegistrationBean   : Mapping filter:
'characterEncodingFilter' to: [/*]
 2018-07-07 14:32:29.389  INFO 4838 --- [ost-startStop-1]
o.s.b.w.servlet.FilterRegistrationBean   : Mapping filter:
'hiddenHttpMethodFilter' to: [/*]
 2018-07-07 14:32:29.389  INFO 4838 --- [ost-startStop-1]
o.s.b.w.servlet.FilterRegistrationBean   : Mapping filter:
'httpPutFormContentFilter' to: [/*]
 2018-07-07 14:32:29.389  INFO 4838 --- [ost-startStop-1]
o.s.b.w.servlet.FilterRegistrationBean   : Mapping filter:
'requestContextFilter' to: [/*]
 2018-07-07 14:32:29.482  INFO 4838 --- [           main]
o.s.w.s.handler.SimpleUrlHandlerMapping  : Mapped URL path [/**/favicon.ico]
onto handler of type [class
org.springframework.web.servlet.resource.ResourceHttpRequestHandler]
 2018-07-07 14:32:29.624  INFO 4838 --- [           main]
s.w.s.m.m.a.RequestMappingHandlerAdapter : Looking for @ControllerAdvice:
org.springframework.boot.web.servlet.context.AnnotationConfigServletWebServer
ApplicationContext@288c63fb: startup date [Sat Jul 07 14:32:28 CEST 2018];
root of context hierarchy
 2018-07-07 14:32:29.689  INFO 4838 --- [           main]
s.w.s.m.m.a.RequestMappingHandlerMapping : Mapped "{[/error]}" onto public
org.springframework.http.ResponseEntity<java.util.Map<java.lang.String,
java.lang.Object>>
org.springframework.boot.autoconfigure.web.servlet.error.BasicErrorController
.error(javax.servlet.http.HttpServletRequest)
 2018-07-07 14:32:29.690  INFO 4838 --- [           main]
s.w.s.m.m.a.RequestMappingHandlerMapping : Mapped
"{[/error],produces=[text/html]}" onto public
org.springframework.web.servlet.ModelAndView
org.springframework.boot.autoconfigure.web.servlet.error.BasicErrorController
.errorHtml(javax.servlet.http.HttpServletRequest,javax.servlet.http.HttpServl
etResponse)
 2018-07-07 14:32:29.714  INFO 4838 --- [           main]
o.s.w.s.handler.SimpleUrlHandlerMapping  : Mapped URL path [/webjars/**] onto
handler of type [class
```

```
org.springframework.web.servlet.resource.ResourceHttpRequestHandler]
 2018-07-07 14:32:29.714  INFO 4838 --- [           main]
o.s.w.s.handler.SimpleUrlHandlerMapping  : Mapped URL path [/**] onto handler
of type [class
org.springframework.web.servlet.resource.ResourceHttpRequestHandler]
 2018-07-07 14:32:29.835  INFO 4838 --- [           main]
o.s.j.e.a.AnnotationMBeanExporter        : Registering beans for JMX exposure
on startup
 2018-07-07 14:32:29.880  INFO 4838 --- [           main]
o.s.b.w.embedded.tomcat.TomcatWebServer  : Tomcat started on port(s): 8080
(http) with context path ''
 2018-07-07 14:32:29.884  INFO 4838 --- [           main]
com.springbook.application.Application   : Started Application in 1.826
seconds (JVM running for 4.227)
```

You have a fully working application that starts an embedded Tomcat on port 8080. It also configures logging to the console.

Spring Boot analyses what is on the class path and will enable functionality based on this. In this case, you have Tomcat on the class path due to the spring-boot-starter-web dependency in the pom.xml:

```
<dependency>
    <groupId>org.springframework.boot</groupId>
    <artifactId>spring-boot-starter-web</artifactId>
</dependency>
```

Properties

Spring Boot lets you configure various parts of your application via the application.properties file. To try this out, add the following line in the file:

```
server.port=8888
```

After restarting the application, the logging output will show that your application now runs on that different port:

```
Tomcat started on port(s): 8888 (http)
```

You can view a list of the most common properties at Appendix A. Common application properties [https://docs.spring.io/spring-boot/docs/current/reference/html/common-application-properties.html] of the Spring Boot reference documentation.

There are two other important ways to configure properties: with the command line or with environment variables

To change the port using the command line, do the following:

```
java -jar application.jar --server.port=8888
```

To change the port with an environment variable, you can define SERVER_PORT and your application will pick this up. Notice how you can use capitals and an underscore in the environment variable and Spring Boot will still pick it up. This feature is called relaxed binding [https://docs.spring.io/spring-boot/docs/current/reference/html/boot-features-external-config.html#boot-features-external-config-relaxed-binding].

See Externalized Configuration [https://docs.spring.io/spring-boot/docs/current/reference/html/boot-features-external-config.html] for all the ways you can configure properties with Spring Boot.

Spring profiles

Spring profiles let you selectively enable or disable parts of your application. The Spring Boot documentation [https://docs.spring.io/spring-boot/docs/current/reference/html/boot-features-profiles.html] says that Spring profiles "provide a way to segregate parts of your application configuration and make it only available in certain environments".

For example, you can have an `EmailGateway` interface with a `LoggingEmailGateway`, `SendGridEmailGateway` and `SmtpEmailGateway` implementations. You could then use the `LoggingEmailGateway` during development, `SmtpEmailGateway` in staging, and `SendGridEmailGateway` for production.

The staging and production environment should be as closely aligned as possible. So this example is more for the purposes of illustration rather than a recommendation of best practice.

Only enabling a class if a profile is active

This code shows how to define a singleton in Spring and have Spring create an instance only if the dev profile is active:

```
@Component
@Profile("dev")
public class LoggingEmailGateway implements EmailGateway {
    ...
}
```

To test this, you must set the active profile when running your application. You can do this by setting spring.profiles.active in application.properties or you can pass it as a program argument. For example:

```
java -jar application.jar --spring.profiles.active=dev
```

 Some IDEs have built-in support for activating profiles. This is a screenshot of the run configuration dialogue of Jetbrains' IntelliJ IDEA:

Spring profile-specific properties

By default, Spring Boot will apply the properties defined in application.properties on the root of the class path. If you want to set specific settings only for when a certain profile is active, you can use the naming convention application-<profileName>.properties.

For example, to set the web listening port to 5000 for production:

application-prod.properties

```
server.port=5000
```

Another common use case for this is specifying the database connection URL since this changes in the various environments your application will run in.

Configure logging

Logging for the production code

Spring Boot uses Logback for logging by default, and logs everything to the console. While this is great when running in your IDE, you might want to log things to a file for staging or production.

To configure this, create a `logback-spring.xml` file:

```xml
<?xml version="1.0" encoding="UTF-8"?>
<configuration>
    <include resource="org/springframework/boot/logging/logback/defaults.xml"/> ①
    <springProfile name="dev,local">②
        <include resource="org/springframework/boot/logging/logback/console-appender.xml" />
        <root level="INFO">
            <appender-ref ref="CONSOLE" />
        </root>
    </springProfile>

    <springProfile name="staging,prod">③
        <include resource="org/springframework/boot/logging/logback/file-appender.xml"/>
        <root level="INFO">
            <appender-ref ref="FILE"/>
        </root>
    </springProfile>
</configuration>
```

① These are the Spring Boot defaults.

② If the Spring profile `dev` or `local` is enabled, then log to console.

③ If the Spring profile `staging` or `prod` is enabled, then log to file.

This is the minimal configuration needed to easily switch between console and file and still allow Spring Boot properties to influence what is logged.

To set the name of the log file, adjust `application-staging.properties` or `application-prod.properties`:

```
logging.file=my-application.log
logging.level.root=INFO
```

Logging for the test code

To configure the logging for the test code, we can rely on the default behaviour of Logback to search for a `logback-test.xml` file on the class path.

By putting this file in `src/test/resources`, it will be first on the class path when the tests are run and used automatically by Logback.

This is a sample file that logs to the console and sets the default level for the loggers of your own application to DEBUG:

```xml
<configuration>
    <appender name="STDOUT" class="ch.qos.logback.core.ConsoleAppender">
        <encoder>
            <pattern>%date{YYYY-MM-dd HH:mm:ss} %level [%thread] %logger{0} - %msg%n%ex</pattern>
        </encoder>
    </appender>

    <root level="WARN">
        <appender-ref ref="STDOUT"/>
    </root>
    <logger name="com.springbook.application"> ①
        <level value="DEBUG"/>
    </logger>
    <logger name="org.hibernate">
        <level value="WARN"/>
    </logger>
    <logger name="org.hibernate.type">
        <level value="WARN"/> <!-- set to TRACE to view parameter binding in queries -->
    </logger>
    <logger name="org.springframework.security">
        <level value="WARN"/>
    </logger>

</configuration>
```

① This configures loggers of `com.springbook.application` and its sub-packages to DEBUG.

Getting Started

If you run `mvn clean install` now, you will get lots of output. If you were to add some logging of your own, it would also show in the Maven output:

```
[INFO] --- maven-surefire-plugin:2.21.0:test (default-test) @ application ---
[INFO]
[INFO] -------------------------------------------------------
[INFO]  T E S T S
[INFO] -------------------------------------------------------
[INFO] Running com.springbook.application.ApplicationTests
14:42:57.455 [main] DEBUG
org.springframework.test.context.junit4.SpringJUnit4ClassRunner -
SpringJUnit4ClassRunner constructor called with [class
com.springbook.application.ApplicationTests]
14:42:57.460 [main] DEBUG org.springframework.test.context.BootstrapUtils -
Instantiating CacheAwareContextLoaderDelegate from class
[org.springframework.test.context.cache.DefaultCacheAwareContextLoaderDelegat
e]

<snip>

  .   ____          _            __ _ _
 /\\ / ___'_ __ _ _(_)_ __  __ _ \ \ \ \
( ( )\___ | '_ | '_| | '_ \/ _` | \ \ \ \
 \\/  ___)| |_)| | | | | || (_| |  ) ) ) )
  '  |____| .__|_| |_|_| |_\__, | / / / /
 =========|_|==============|___/=/_/_/_/
 :: Spring Boot ::        (v2.0.3.RELEASE)

2018-07-07 14:42:58.023  INFO 9617 --- [           main]
c.s.application.ApplicationTests         : Starting ApplicationTests on Wims-
MacBook-Pro.local with PID 9617 (started by wdb in
/Users/wdb/Projects/spring-boot-book/src/example-code/chapter02/01 -
Generated project)
2018-07-07 14:42:58.025  INFO 9617 --- [           main]
c.s.application.ApplicationTests         : No active profile set, falling
back to default profiles: default
2018-07-07 14:42:58.066  INFO 9617 --- [           main]
o.s.w.c.s.GenericWebApplicationContext   : Refreshing
org.springframework.web.context.support.GenericWebApplicationContext@53aac487
: startup date [Sat Jul 07 14:42:58 CEST 2018]; root of context hierarchy
2018-07-07 14:42:58.942  INFO 9617 --- [           main]
o.s.w.s.handler.SimpleUrlHandlerMapping  : Mapped URL path [/**/favicon.ico]
onto handler of type [class
org.springframework.web.servlet.resource.ResourceHttpRequestHandler]
2018-07-07 14:42:59.115  INFO 9617 --- [           main]
s.w.s.m.m.a.RequestMappingHandlerAdapter : Looking for @ControllerAdvice:
org.springframework.web.context.support.GenericWebApplicationContext@53aac487
: startup date [Sat Jul 07 14:42:58 CEST 2018]; root of context hierarchy
2018-07-07 14:42:59.172  INFO 9617 --- [           main]
s.w.s.m.m.a.RequestMappingHandlerMapping : Mapped "{[/error]}" onto public
org.springframework.http.ResponseEntity<java.util.Map<java.lang.String,
```

```
java.lang.Object>>
org.springframework.boot.autoconfigure.web.servlet.error.BasicErrorController
.error(javax.servlet.http.HttpServletRequest)
2018-07-07 14:42:59.173  INFO 9617 --- [           main] 
s.w.s.m.m.a.RequestMappingHandlerMapping : Mapped 
"{[/error],produces=[text/html]}" onto public 
org.springframework.web.servlet.ModelAndView 
org.springframework.boot.autoconfigure.web.servlet.error.BasicErrorController
.errorHtml(javax.servlet.http.HttpServletRequest,javax.servlet.http.HttpServl
etResponse)
2018-07-07 14:42:59.191  INFO 9617 --- [           main] 
o.s.w.s.handler.SimpleUrlHandlerMapping  : Mapped URL path [/webjars/**] onto 
handler of type [class 
org.springframework.web.servlet.resource.ResourceHttpRequestHandler]
2018-07-07 14:42:59.191  INFO 9617 --- [           main] 
o.s.w.s.handler.SimpleUrlHandlerMapping  : Mapped URL path [/**] onto handler 
of type [class 
org.springframework.web.servlet.resource.ResourceHttpRequestHandler]
2018-07-07 14:42:59.302  INFO 9617 --- [           main] 
c.s.application.ApplicationTests         : Started ApplicationTests in 1.506 
seconds (JVM running for 2.194)
[INFO] Tests run: 1, Failures: 0, Errors: 0, Skipped: 0, Time elapsed: 2.064 
s - in com.springbook.application.ApplicationTests
2018-07-07 14:42:59.390  INFO 9617 --- [       Thread-2] 
o.s.w.c.s.GenericWebApplicationContext   : Closing 
org.springframework.web.context.support.GenericWebApplicationContext@53aac487
: startup date [Sat Jul 07 14:42:58 CEST 2018]; root of context hierarchy
[INFO] 
[INFO] Results:
[INFO] 
[INFO] Tests run: 1, Failures: 0, Errors: 0, Skipped: 0
```

You probably don't want the output of your tests to appear when running with Maven. To have Maven put all the output in a file, use the following configuration for the Maven Surefire Plugin [http://maven.apache.org/surefire/maven-surefire-plugin/]:

```
<plugin>
    <groupId>org.apache.maven.plugins</groupId>
    <artifactId>maven-surefire-plugin</artifactId>
    <configuration>
        <redirectTestOutputToFile>true</redirectTestOutputToFile> ①
        <printSummary>false</printSummary>
    </configuration>
</plugin>
```

① Set the `redirectTestOutputToFile` to `true` so Surefire will put the output of each test in a separate file.

Source code for the book

If you ever get stuck following along, you can refer to the full source code on GitHub: https://github.com/wimdeblauwe/spring-boot-building-api-backend

CHAPTER THREE
CopsBoot

Explanation of the sample project

The sample application upon which the examples in this this book are based is entirely fictional but will serve well to demonstrate all the important concepts.

The application, called CopsBoot, supports a police force in their daily work. It allows officers on the road to interact with the server via a mobile application. Through the mobile app, officers can report crimes and attach images to their reports.

This book will not deal with the development of the mobile application itself but will show how the API will work using Postman [https://www.getpostman.com/]. Spring REST Docs [https://projects.spring.io/spring-restdocs/] will generate some beautiful documentation that should contain all the info an app developer would need to get started.

Generating the project skeleton

To get started, use Spring Initializr at https://start.spring.io with the following values:

Property	Value
Build system	Maven Project
Programming language	Java
Spring Boot version	2.0.3
Artifact Group	com.example
Artifact	copsboot
Search for dependencies	Web, Security, JPA, H2

Unzip the generated .zip file to a location of your choice.

The dependencies section of the pom.xml will look like this:

```xml
<dependencies>
    <dependency>
        <groupId>org.springframework.boot</groupId>
        <artifactId>spring-boot-starter-data-jpa</artifactId>①
    </dependency>
    <dependency>
        <groupId>org.springframework.boot</groupId>
        <artifactId>spring-boot-starter-security</artifactId>②
    </dependency>
    <dependency>
        <groupId>org.springframework.boot</groupId>
        <artifactId>spring-boot-starter-web</artifactId>③
    </dependency>

    <dependency>
        <groupId>com.h2database</groupId>
        <artifactId>h2</artifactId> ④
        <scope>runtime</scope>
    </dependency>

    <dependency>
        <groupId>org.springframework.boot</groupId>
        <artifactId>spring-boot-starter-test</artifactId>
        <scope>test</scope>
    </dependency>
    <dependency>
        <groupId>org.springframework.security</groupId>
        <artifactId>spring-security-test</artifactId>⑤
        <scope>test</scope>
    </dependency>
</dependencies>
```

① JPA is the Java Persistence API. This starter pulls in Hibernate, which you will use to persist your entities to the database.

② This adds support for Spring Security so you can have authorization and authentication.

③ This adds support for web and REST controllers for building your API.

④ H2 is an in-memory database that will be used for running the application locally and for unit testing.

⑤ These are helper classes for testing your Spring Security configuration.

CHAPTER FOUR

User Management

The first thing to add your application is user management and security.

User domain

Create a class User to hold all properties of your users. For now, start out simple and use only the following properties:

Property	Description
Name	The full name of the user.
Email	The email address of the user, which will also serve as the username for login.
Password	The user's password.
Role	The user's role in the system, which defines what a user can and can't do.

Start with the following code for User:

User.java

```java
package com.example.copsboot.user;

import java.util.Set;
import java.util.UUID;

public class User {
    private UUID id;
    private String email;
    private String password;
    private Set<UserRole> roles;

    public User(UUID id, String email, String password, Set<UserRole> roles)
    {
        this.id = id;
        this.email = email;
        this.password = password;
        this.roles = roles;
    }

    public UUID getId() {
        return id;
    }

    public String getEmail() {
        return email;
    }

    public String getPassword() {
        return password;
    }

    public Set<UserRole> getRoles() {
        return roles;
    }
}
```

UserRole defines the roles of users in the application:

UserRole.java

```java
package com.example.copsboot.user;

public enum UserRole {
    OFFICER,
    CAPTAIN,
    ADMIN
}
```

To keep the example simple, create only three roles:

- Officer is a police officer who does the field work.
- Captain is the boss of the officers.
- Admin is an administrative role that has access to all parts of the application.

Notice how we use the com.example.copsboot.user package for our domain class. Some developers prefer packages by layer, which groups types of similar classes like domain classes in a domain package, services in a service package, etc. Using packages by feature, however, makes the core abstractions of the project immediately visible on the package tree.

To persist your first domain class using Spring Boot Data JPA, you must add some annotations from the Java Persistence API (JPA) specification:

```
package com.example.copsboot.user;

import javax.persistence.*;
import javax.validation.constraints.NotNull;
import java.util.Set;
import java.util.UUID;

@Entity ①
@Table(name = "copsboot_user") ②
public class User {
    @Id
    private UUID id; ③

    private String email;
    private String password;

    @ElementCollection(fetch = FetchType.EAGER)
    @Enumerated(EnumType.STRING)
    @NotNull
    private Set<UserRole> roles; ④

    protected User() { ⑤

    }

    public User(UUID id, String email, String password, Set<UserRole> roles) {
        this.id = id;
        this.email = email;
        this.password = password;
        this.roles = roles;
    }
```

① `@Entity` marks the class as a persistable entity for JPA.

② The `@Table` annotation is optional. It allows you to explicitly set the name to be used for the database table. If you do not specify a name, Spring Boot will convert the name of the class to snake_case.

③ The `id` field is annotated with `@Id` to mark it as a primary key of the entity.

④ The `roles` field is a collection of enum values. `@Enumerated(EnumType.STRING)` ensures the enum values are stored as string values.

⑤ Hibernate needs a no-argument constructor, so this adds one. It does not need to be public, so this keeps it `protected`.

This application uses "early primary key" generation. This means that it does not rely on the database to provide a primary key, but first creates a primary key, which passes into the constructor of your User object. The main advantages of this are that you never have "incomplete" objects and it makes it easier to implement equals.

User repository

The actual persistence happens through a repository. The heavy lifting for the repository pattern [https://martinfowler.com/eaaCatalog/repository.html] has been implemented in Spring Data. Using it is as simple as defining an interface that extends from CrudRepository:

```
package com.example.copsboot.user;

import org.springframework.data.repository.CrudRepository;

import java.util.UUID;

public interface UserRepository extends CrudRepository<User, UUID> {
}
```

By creating this interface, you have a repository at run time that allows you to save, edit, delete, and find User entities.

To check that everything works, create a test for it:

User Management

```
package com.example.copsboot.user;

import org.junit.Test;
import org.junit.runner.RunWith;
import org.springframework.beans.factory.annotation.Autowired;
import org.springframework.boot.test.autoconfigure.orm.jpa.DataJpaTest;
import org.springframework.test.context.junit4.SpringRunner;

import java.util.HashSet;
import java.util.UUID;

import static org.assertj.core.api.Assertions.assertThat;

@RunWith(SpringRunner.class) ①
@DataJpaTest ②
public class UserRepositoryTest {

    @Autowired
    private UserRepository repository; ③

    @Test
    public void testStoreUser() { ④
        HashSet<UserRole> roles = new HashSet<>();
        roles.add(UserRole.OFFICER);
        User user = repository.save(new User(UUID.randomUUID(), ⑤
                                    "alex.foley@beverly-hills.com",
                                    "my-secret-pwd",
                                    roles));
        assertThat(user).isNotNull(); ⑥

        assertThat(repository.count()).isEqualTo(1L); ⑦
    }
}
```

① You need to annotate the JUnit test class with @RunWith(SpringRunner.class) to enable the testing support of Spring Boot.

② @DataJpaTest instructs the testing support to start only the part of the application responsible for everything related to JPA.

③ Inject the UserRepository so you can use it in the unit test.

④ This is the method that contains your test.

⑤ Save the User entity in the database here.

⑥ The object returned from the save method of the repository should return a non-null object.

⑦ If you count the number of User entities in the database, you should have one.

> The act of starting only part of the application context in a unit test is what Spring calls test slicing [https://spring.io/blog/2016/04/15/testing-improvements-in-spring-boot-1-4]. Doing it makes the unit tests faster and more focused as fewer components need to be bootstrapped.

The unit test uses AssertJ [http://joel-costigliola.github.io/assertj/] as an assertions framework. Its tagline is "fluent assertions for Java" and that is exactly what it is and why I like it so much. To use it, update pom.xml with the extra dependency:

```
<dependency>
    <groupId>org.assertj</groupId>
    <artifactId>assertj-core</artifactId>
    <scope>test</scope>
</dependency>
```

> You don't have to specify a version for AssertJ as the base pom of Spring Boot has a version specified for it.

You need a database before you can run the test. For tests like these, the easiest way to get one is by putting the H2 database on the classpath. If we do that, Spring Boot will create an instance of it and use it in the test. This dependency should normally already be present in the pom.xml:

```
<dependency>
    <groupId>com.h2database</groupId>
    <artifactId>h2</artifactId>
    <scope>runtime</scope> ①
</dependency>
```

① The dependency has been added with runtime scope (as opposed to test scope) as you will also start the application itself with H2 if you run it with the dev profile.

Running the test should succeed:

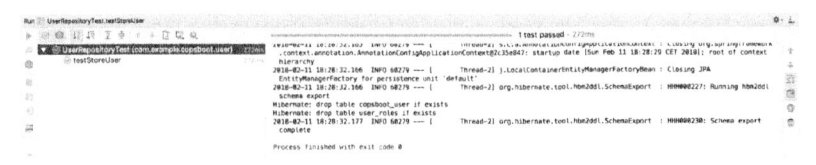

User-domain refactoring

You can now save your User entities in the database. However, implementing the following changes can improve the maintainability of the code:

1. Use a dedicated class for the primary key.
2. Extract a superclass for all entities so that the primary key is defined in a consistent way.
3. Centralize the primary-key generation in the repository.

Dedicated primary-key class

Most examples use either a long or a UUID as the primary key for an entity. One alternative, as described in *Implementing Domain Drive Design* [https://www.amazon.com/Implementing-Domain-Driven-Design-Vaughn-Vernon/dp/0321834577] by Vaughn Vernon, is to use a dedicated class for primary keys. This has the following advantages:

- It more clearly expresses the intent. If a variable is of type UserId, it is clear what you are are talking about, as opposed to a simple long or UUID.
- It is impossible to assign a value that is a UserId to an OrderId or a BookId. This reduces the chance of putting a wrong ID somewhere.
- If you want to change from UUID to long or vice versa for the primary key, you will be able to do so with minimal changes to the application code.

Create this AbstractEntityId class as the basis for all the ID classes in your application:

AbstractEntityId.java

```
package com.example.orm.jpa;

import com.example.util.ArtifactForFramework;

import javax.persistence.MappedSuperclass;
import java.io.Serializable;
import java.util.Objects;

import static com.google.common.base.MoreObjects.toStringHelper;
```

```java
@MappedSuperclass
public abstract class AbstractEntityId<T extends Serializable> implements
Serializable, EntityId<T> {
    private T id;

    @ArtifactForFramework
    protected AbstractEntityId() {
    }

    protected AbstractEntityId(T id) {
        this.id = Objects.requireNonNull(id);
    }

    @Override
    public T getId() {
        return id;
    }

    @Override
    public String asString() {
        return id.toString();
    }

    @Override
    public boolean equals(Object o) {
        boolean result = false;

        if (this == o) {
            result = true;
        } else if (o instanceof AbstractEntityId) {
            AbstractEntityId other = (AbstractEntityId) o;
            result = Objects.equals(id, other.id);
        }

        return result;
    }

    @Override
    public int hashCode() {
        return Objects.hash(id);
    }

    @Override
    public String toString() {
        return toStringHelper(this)
                .add("id", id)
                .toString();
    }
}
```

The empty constructor is annotated with
`@ArtifactForFramework`. Create this annotation to indicate
that the constructor is solely there for a framework that
needs it but is not intended to be used by the application
itself.

The code of the annotation itself is simple:

```
import java.lang.annotation.Retention;
import java.lang.annotation.RetentionPolicy;

@Retention(value = RetentionPolicy.SOURCE)
public @interface ArtifactForFramework {
}
```

An extra benefit is that in IntelliJ IDEA, for example, you
can indicate that elements annotated with this
annotation should not be marked as unused.

To make `AbstractEntityId` compile, you need to add Guava as a dependency:

```xml
<dependency>
    <groupId>com.google.guava</groupId>
    <artifactId>guava</artifactId>
    <version>${guava.version}</version>
</dependency>
```

Next, define `AbstractEntity`. This will be the base class for your entities and ensures that they will use your `EntityId`:

AbstractEntity.java

```java
package com.example.orm.jpa;

import com.example.util.ArtifactForFramework;

import javax.persistence.EmbeddedId;
import javax.persistence.MappedSuperclass;
import java.util.Objects;

import static com.google.common.base.MoreObjects.toStringHelper;
import static com.google.common.base.Preconditions.checkNotNull;

/**
 * Abstract super class for entities. We are assuming that early primary key
```

```java
 * generation will be used.
 *
 * @param <T> the type of {@link EntityId} that will be used for this entity
 */
@MappedSuperclass
public abstract class AbstractEntity<T extends EntityId> implements Entity<T>
{

    @EmbeddedId
    private T id;


    @ArtifactForFramework
    protected AbstractEntity() {
    }

    public AbstractEntity(T id) {
        this.id = checkNotNull(id);
    }


    @Override
    public T getId() {
        return id;
    }

    @Override
    public boolean equals(Object obj) {
        boolean result = false;

        if (this == obj) {
            result = true;
        } else if (obj instanceof AbstractEntity) {
            AbstractEntity other = (AbstractEntity) obj;
            result = Objects.equals(id, other.id);
        }

        return result;
    }

    @Override
    public int hashCode() {
        return Objects.hash(id);
    }

    @Override
    public String toString() {
        return toStringHelper(this)
                .add("id", id)
                .toString();
    }
}
```

For completeness, here is the interface implementation of EntityId and Entity:

EntityId.java

```
package com.example.orm.jpa;

import java.io.Serializable;

/**
 * Interface for primary keys of entities.
 *
 * @param <T> the underlying type of the entity id
 */
public interface EntityId<T> extends Serializable {

    T getId();

    String asString(); ①
}
```

① The asString method returns the ID as a string representation, for use in an URL for example. You are not using toString because that is usually for debugging purposes while you will need to use this as part of your application logic.

Entity.java

```
package com.example.orm.jpa;

/**
 * Interface for entity objects.
 *
 * @param <T> the type of {@link EntityId} that will be used in this entity
 */
public interface Entity<T extends EntityId> {

    T getId();
}
```

With all this in place, you can now refactor your User class. First, create a UserId:

41

UserId.java

```
package com.example.copsboot.user;

import com.example.orm.jpa.AbstractEntityId;

import java.util.UUID;

public class UserId extends AbstractEntityId<UUID> {

    protected UserId() { ①

    }

    public UserId(UUID id) { ②
        super(id);
    }
}
```

① Hibernate needs the protected no-args constructor to work.

② This is the constructor that the application code should use.

In the User class itself, you can remove the id field and its getter. The constructor just calls super instead. This is how it looks after the refactoring:

```
@Entity
@Table(name = "copsboot_user")
public class User extends AbstractEntity<UserId> {
```

With the following constructor:

```
    public User(UserId id, String email, String password, Set<UserRole>
roles) {
        super(id);
        this.email = email;
        this.password = password;
        this.roles = roles;
    }
```

Centralize primary-key generation

In your unit test, you manually created the primary key by calling UUID.randomUUID(). This could be fine for a UUID, but certainly not if you want to use long, for example. For this reason, add a method on the UserRepository that will give you the "next" ID to use if you want to create an entity.

Since `UserRepository` is an interface, you need to do some additional work to make this possible. To get started, you need to create a `UserRepositoryCustom` interface:

```
package com.example.copsboot.user;

public interface UserRepositoryCustom {
    UserId nextId();
}
```

The `nextId` method will return a new `UserId` instance each time it is called. Step 2 adds this interface to the `UserRepository` interface:

```
public interface UserRepository extends CrudRepository<User, UUID>,
UserRepositoryCustom {
}
```

Step 3 creates a `UserRepositoryImpl` class that implements the `UserRepositoryCustom` interface method:

```
package com.example.copsboot.user;

import com.example.orm.jpa.UniqueIdGenerator;

import java.util.UUID;

public class UserRepositoryImpl implements UserRepositoryCustom {
    private final UniqueIdGenerator<UUID> generator;

    public UserRepositoryImpl(UniqueIdGenerator<UUID> generator) {
        this.generator = generator;
    }

    @Override
    public UserId nextId() {
        return new UserId(generator.getNextUniqueId());
    }
}
```

When the application runs, Spring Data will combine your own `UserRepositoryImpl` code with Spring Data's `CrudRepository` code so the methods from both `UserRepositoryCustom` and `CrudRepository` are available everywhere you inject a `UserRepository`.

43

The generation of the unique UUID is put behind the UniqueIdGenerator. This might seem like a bit overkill for the UUID case but you certainly need it if you want to use long values. You might want to get them from the database or maybe from some distributed component that can hand out unique IDs across connected JVMs. In that case, having this generation centralized in the UniqueIdGenerator is a big plus.

Updating the unit test

The test method itself now needs to change to use the nextId method from the repository:

```
@Test
public void testStoreUser() {
    HashSet<UserRole> roles = new HashSet<>();
    roles.add(UserRole.OFFICER);
    User user = repository.save(new User(repository.nextId(),
                                    "alex.foley@beverly-hills.com",
                                    "my-secret-pwd",
                                    roles));
    assertThat(user).isNotNull();

    assertThat(repository.count()).isEqualTo(1L);
}
```

However, this is not enough, as you quickly see when you try to run the test:

```
java.lang.IllegalStateException: Failed to load ApplicationContext
```

Digging a bit more in the stacktrace will reveal this:

```
org.springframework.beans.factory.NoSuchBeanDefinitionException: No
qualifying bean of type
'com.example.orm.jpa.UniqueIdGenerator<java.util.UUID>' available: expected
at least 1 bean which qualifies as autowire candidate.
```

The cause of the error is straightforward. Your UserRepositoryImpl needs a UniqueIDGenerator for constructor injection, but there does not seem to be an instance in the application context. Spring Boot will not create an instance of UniqueIdGenerator because you did not ask it to.

You could annotate InMemoryUniqueIdGenerator with @Component, but there is a different way especially for unit tests. You can create a static inner class in your unit-test class and annotate it with @TestConfiguration. You can then use @Bean annotated methods to define singletons that should be available in the unit test. For your test, that looks like this:

UserRepositoryTest.java

```
    @TestConfiguration
    static class TestConfig {
        @Bean
        public UniqueIdGenerator<UUID> generator() {
            return new InMemoryUniqueIdGenerator();
        }
    }
```

After this, your unit test will be green.

As a final step, you also need to make such a bean available in your application. To do this, add the same bean declaration to CopsbootApplication.java:

```
@Bean
public UniqueIdGenerator<UUID> uniqueIdGenerator() {
    return new InMemoryUniqueIdGenerator();
}
```

Summary

You have seen how to store an entity using Spring Data JPA and how to test it.

CHAPTER FIVE

REST API Security

Spring Security OAuth2

The mobile application will use OAuth2 for security. If you are not familiar with OAuth2, you can read a good introduction to it at https://medium.com/@darutk/the-simplest-guide-to-oauth-2-0-8c71bd9a15bb

Let's allow authentication using OAuth2 password flow. In this flow, you validate the client application that does the request, as well as the user. With OAuth2, you use a client secret and client ID to validate the client application along with a username and password to validate the user. In exchange, you get an access token to use for all future requests towards the API (until the access token expires).

Here's an example of a request to get an access token:

```
curl -i \
  -X POST \
  -H 'Content-Type: application/x-www-form-urlencoded' \
  -u the-client-id:the-client-secret \
  -d 'grant_type=password&username=the-user-name&password=the-users-password&client_id=the-client-id&client_secret=the-client-secret' \
  http://localhost:8080/oauth/token
```

> ⚠️ OAuth2 must run over HTTPS to be secure. Always use HTTPS in production!

The server should return a response similar to this:

```
HTTP/1.1 200 OK

{
  "access_token": "4ff47dcc-c00a-4604-905d-de5708d13ce8",
  "token_type": "bearer",
  "refresh_token": "d709ff89-3892-4416-a227-8dd8e4152ebc",
  "expires_in": 43199,
  "scope": "server"
}
```

This example uses Spring Security OAuth2 AutoConfigure to implement this. Start with adding the needed dependency to pom.xml:

```
<dependency>
    <groupId>org.springframework.security.oauth.boot</groupId>
    <artifactId>spring-security-oauth2-autoconfigure</artifactId>
    <version>2.0.1.RELEASE</version>
</dependency>
```

To make things clear and the security configuration simpler, all REST API endpoints will be under /api. If you would want to add a CMS, for example, in the same Spring Boot application, you could serve that at /cms or /admin.

OAuth has two parts:

- The authorization server is responsible for the authorization of the client application and the users.

- The resource server is responsible for defining what parts of the application are accessible by the different types of authenticated and unauthenticated users.

To configure the authorization server, create the following class:

```
@Configuration
@EnableAuthorizationServer ①
protected static class AuthorizationServerConfiguration extends
AuthorizationServerConfigurerAdapter {

    @Autowired
    private AuthenticationManager authenticationManager;

    @Autowired
    private UserDetailsService userDetailsService; ②

    @Autowired
    private PasswordEncoder passwordEncoder; ③

    @Autowired
    private TokenStore tokenStore; ④

    @Override
    public void configure(AuthorizationServerSecurityConfigurer security)
throws Exception {
        security.passwordEncoder(passwordEncoder); ③
    }

    @Override
    public void configure(ClientDetailsServiceConfigurer clients) throws
Exception {
        clients.inMemory() ⑤
                .withClient("copsboot-mobile-client") ⑥
                .authorizedGrantTypes("password", "refresh_token") ⑦
                .scopes("mobile_app") ⑧
                .resourceIds(RESOURCE_ID)
                .secret(passwordEncoder.encode("ccUyb6vS4S8nxfbKPCrN")); ⑨
    }

    @Override
    public void configure(AuthorizationServerEndpointsConfigurer endpoints)
throws Exception {
        endpoints.tokenStore(tokenStore)
                .authenticationManager(authenticationManager)
                .userDetailsService(userDetailsService);
    }
}
```

① The `@EnableAuthorizationServer` annotation ensures that you have an authorization server started.

② `UserDetailsService` is the contact point between your application and Spring Security. You will have to create a class that implements this interface, which will use the previously created `UserRepository` to know what users you have in your application.

REST API Security

③ You obviously should not store user passwords in plain text. This example uses an implementation of `PasswordEncoder` to encrypt passwords when storing them in the database. `PasswordEncoder` hashes the password so that there is no way to recover the original password, even when the complete database leaks out. Spring Security needs access to the same class to be able to validate passwords.

④ The `TokenStore` is what Spring will use to store the generated access tokens.

⑤ You define one client application that will be allowed to get an access token in memory. Since you only have one mobile app for now, you don't need anything more elaborate. You may define this in the database if you want. You would then use `clients.jdbc(dataSource)`.

⑥ Hard-code the client ID for authentication of the client application to `copsboot-mobile-client`.

⑦ This has to be "password" to allow password flow using the defined client application. Also add "refresh_token" so that the client application can use the refresh token to get a new access token.

⑧ The scopes allow you to define what "part" of the application is allowed by the received token. Let's not do anything based on that value for now, so its exact value does not really matter.

⑨ This defines the client secret to authenticate the client application.

Before seeing how to get to the various instances that are injected here, take a look at the resource-server configuration:

```
@Configuration
@EnableResourceServer ①
@EnableGlobalMethodSecurity(prePostEnabled = true, securedEnabled = true)
protected static class ResourceServerConfiguration extends
ResourceServerConfigurerAdapter {

    @Override
    public void configure(ResourceServerSecurityConfigurer resources) throws Exception {
        resources.resourceId(RESOURCE_ID);
    }

    @Override
    public void configure(HttpSecurity http) throws Exception {

        http.authorizeRequests()
            .antMatchers(HttpMethod.OPTIONS, "/api/**").permitAll() ②
            .and()
            .antMatcher("/api/**").authorizeRequests()
            .anyRequest().authenticated(); ③
    }
}
```

① The `@EnableResourceServer` annotation ensures that you have a resource server.

② You define via the fluent API that any `OPTIONS` request to any sub-path of `/api` is allowed by everybody. This allows a client to issue a so-called "preflight request". See https://stackoverflow.com/questions/15381105/cors-what-is-the-motivation-behind-introducing-preflight-requests for more info on that. This is something that the Angular framework, for example, does by default.

③ This defines that any request to `/api` should be authenticated (unless it is an `OPTIONS` request).

UserDetailsService

To tie your application to Spring Security, you need to implement the `UserDetailsService` interface from Spring Security. It has only one method [https://github.com/spring-projects/spring-security/blob/master/core/src/main/java/org/springframework/security/core/userdetails/UserDetailsService.java] (comments omitted):

org.springframework.security.core.userdetails.UserDetailsService.java

```
public interface UserDetailsService {
    UserDetails loadUserByUsername(String username) throws UsernameNotFoundException;
}
```

> The interface explicitly declares the UsernameNotFoundException, although that is not needed since it is a RuntimeException (per Spring's convention of using a RuntimeException for everything).
>
> Most likely, this is done to clearly state what kind of Exception the Spring Security framework expects to receive when you implement this interface and the user cannot be found.

Spring Security will pass in a username and we need to provide a UserDetails implementation if there is such a user in our application. If not, we throw a UsernameNotFoundException.

To make such a class for our application, we need two things:

- a finder method to get a user based on username (which is the email address in our case), and
- an implementation of UserDetails that contains information on the found user.

Find user by email address

Finding the user by email address is extremely simple since you are using Spring Data JPA. This library allows you to define query methods [https://docs.spring.io/spring-data/jpa/docs/current/reference/html/#repositories.query-methods.details] in the repository for which you don't have to provide an implementation. By simply following the naming convention of findByPropertyName, Spring Data will properly query your database.

In your case, the code looks like this:

```
public interface UserRepository extends CrudRepository<User, UUID>, UserRepositoryCustom {
    Optional<User> findByEmailIgnoreCase(String email);
}
```

53

You could have used findByEmail as well, but chose findByEmailIgnoreCase to make the query case insensitive. As the return type, use Optional<User>, since the user might or might not be there. You could also use User. In that case, Spring Data would return a null reference when there is no user with the given email address.

> *Optional*
>
> Since Java 8, Java has an Optional type that is intended to be used as a return type of a method. It signals to the caller that an actual value might be present or not. It helps to avoid having a NullPointerException by making it explicit that a value might not be there. See "Guide to Java 8 Optional" [http://www.baeldung.com/java-optional] for more info.

To make sure this finder method works, add three unit tests for it:

UserRepositoryTest.java

```java
    @Test
    public void testFindByEmail() {
        User user = Users.newRandomOfficer();
        repository.save(user);
        Optional<User> optional =
repository.findByEmailIgnoreCase(user.getEmail());

        assertThat(optional).isNotEmpty()
                            .contains(user);
    }

    @Test
    public void testFindByEmailIgnoringCase() {
        User user = Users.newRandomOfficer();
        repository.save(user);
        Optional<User> optional =
repository.findByEmailIgnoreCase(user.getEmail()

.toUpperCase(Locale.US));

        assertThat(optional).isNotEmpty()
                            .contains(user);
    }

    @Test
    public void testFindByEmail_unknownEmail() {
        User user = Users.newRandomOfficer();
        repository.save(user);
        Optional<User> optional =
repository.findByEmailIgnoreCase("will.not@find.me");

        assertThat(optional).isEmpty();
    }
```

Create a new class called Users to support the unit test. This is a factory class that makes it easy to create random users for testing:

Users.java

```java
package com.example.copsboot.user;

import org.springframework.security.crypto.bcrypt.BCryptPasswordEncoder;
import org.springframework.security.crypto.password.PasswordEncoder;

import java.util.UUID;

public class Users {
    private static final PasswordEncoder PASSWORD_ENCODER = new BCryptPasswordEncoder();
```

```
    public static final String OFFICER_EMAIL = "officer@example.com";
    public static final String OFFICER_PASSWORD = "officer";
    public static final String CAPTAIN_EMAIL = "captain@example.com";
    public static final String CAPTAIN_PASSWORD = "captain";

    private static User OFFICER = User.createOfficer(newRandomId(),
                                                     OFFICER_EMAIL,
PASSWORD_ENCODER.encode(OFFICER_PASSWORD));

    private static User CAPTAIN = User.createCaptain(newRandomId(),
                                                     CAPTAIN_EMAIL,
PASSWORD_ENCODER.encode(CAPTAIN_PASSWORD));


    public static UserId newRandomId() {
        return new UserId(UUID.randomUUID());
    }

    public static User newRandomOfficer() {
        return newRandomOfficer(newRandomId());
    }

    public static User newRandomOfficer(UserId userId) {
        String uniqueId = userId.asString().substring(0, 5);
        return User.createOfficer(userId,
                                  "user-" + uniqueId +
                                        "@example.com",
                                  PASSWORD_ENCODER.encode("user"));
    }

    public static User officer() {
        return OFFICER;
    }

    public static User captain() {
        return CAPTAIN;
    }

    private Users() {
    }
}
```

> Using BCryptPasswordEncoder here does not mean your passwords are safe, as decompilation of the class will reveal those password strings. But since this is just for testing, that is not a problem here.

I will always create a factory class for each entity in an application. The advantage of having a factory class like that is twofold:

- You centralize the creation, so that if the constructor of User changes, you just have to change it in the Users class itself as opposed to each and every unit test that uses that entity.
- The method names make it describe the kind of user object you are creating.

UserDetails implementation

The return type of the method in UserDetailsService needs to be an implementation of org.springframework.security.core.userdetails.UserDetails. This interface has seven methods, which you can quite easily implement if you want to. But an even easier option is to create a subclass of org.springframework.security.core.userdetails.User with a constructor that takes an instance of your application's User object:

```
package com.example.copsboot.infrastructure.security;

import com.example.copsboot.user.User;
import com.example.copsboot.user.UserId;
import com.example.copsboot.user.UserRole;
import org.springframework.security.core.authority.SimpleGrantedAuthority;

import java.util.Collection;
import java.util.Set;
import java.util.stream.Collectors;

public class ApplicationUserDetails extends
org.springframework.security.core.userdetails.User { ①

    private static final String ROLE_PREFIX = "ROLE_";

    private final UserId userId;

    public ApplicationUserDetails(User user) {
        super(user.getEmail(), user.getPassword(),
createAuthorities(user.getRoles()));
        this.userId = user.getId();
    }

    public UserId getUserId() {
        return userId;
    }

    private static Collection<SimpleGrantedAuthority>
createAuthorities(Set<UserRole> roles) {
        return roles.stream()
                    .map(userRole -> new SimpleGrantedAuthority(ROLE_PREFIX +
userRole.name()))
                    .collect(Collectors.toSet());
    }
}
```

① You need to fully qualify org.springframework.security.core.userdetails.User since you already import com.example.copsboot.user.User.

The only actual logic you need to implement is the conversion from UserRole to SimpleGrantedAuthority, which ensures that Spring Security is aware of the role of each user.

REST API Security

Alternative implementation

You could have instead directly implemented `UserDetails` in the User object:

```
public class User extends AbstractEntity<UserId>
    implements UserDetails {
```

If you do that, you need to be aware of three caveats:

1. `getAuthorities()` should return the authorities sorted. Check the source code of `org.springframework.security.core.userdetails.User` to see exactly how to do this.

2. You need to make `AbstractEntity` implement `Serializable` (because the `UserDetails` interface implements it) and thus all `AbstractEntity` classes going forward will have to take that into account.

3. Spring Security caches the `UserDetails` object so you need to be careful if you use the object you get from `@AuthenticationPrincipal User user` in a `Controller`.

ApplicationUserDetailsService

Now that you have your finder method and the `ApplicationUserDetails` class, you can implement `ApplicationUserDetailsService`:

59

```
package com.example.copsboot.infrastructure.security;

import com.example.copsboot.user.User;
import com.example.copsboot.user.UserRepository;
import org.springframework.beans.factory.annotation.Autowired;
import org.springframework.security.core.userdetails.UserDetails;
import org.springframework.security.core.userdetails.UserDetailsService;
import org.springframework.security.core.userdetails.UsernameNotFoundException;
import org.springframework.stereotype.Service;

import static java.lang.String.format;

@Service ①
public class ApplicationUserDetailsService implements UserDetailsService {

    private final UserRepository userRepository;

    @Autowired
    public ApplicationUserDetailsService(UserRepository userRepository) { ②
        this.userRepository = userRepository;
    }

    @Override
    public UserDetails loadUserByUsername(String username) {
        User user = userRepository.findByEmailIgnoreCase(username) ③
                                  .orElseThrow(() -> new
UsernameNotFoundException( ④

String.format("User with email %s could not be found",

username)));
        return new ApplicationUserDetails(user); ⑤
    }
}
```

① `@Service` tells Spring's component scanning to create a singleton instance of this class.

② You inject `UserRepository` into your class since you need it.

③ Use the `findByEmailIgnoreCase` method to find the user.

④ Since you get an `Optional`, you can use `orElseThrow` to return the value if it is present or throw an exception if it is not present.

⑤ Wrap your `User` object in the `ApplicationUserDetails` object and return it for Spring Security to further handle it.

The code is straightforward so your unit test can be quite simple as well. You have two code paths to test:

REST API Security

- If the requested username/email address exists, return the correct ApplicationUserDetails object.
- The username is unknown, the code throws UsernameNotFoundException.

```
package com.example.copsboot.infrastructure.security;


import com.example.copsboot.user.UserRepository;
import com.example.copsboot.user.Users;
import org.junit.Test;
import org.springframework.security.core.GrantedAuthority;
import org.springframework.security.core.userdetails.UserDetails;
import
org.springframework.security.core.userdetails.UsernameNotFoundException;

import java.util.Optional;

import static org.assertj.core.api.Assertions.assertThat;
import static org.assertj.core.api.Assertions.assertThatThrownBy;
import static org.mockito.Matchers.anyString;
import static org.mockito.Mockito.mock;
import static org.mockito.Mockito.when;

public class ApplicationUserDetailsServiceTest {

    @Test
    public void givenExistingUsername_whenLoadingUser_userIsReturned() {
        UserRepository repository = mock(UserRepository.class);
        ApplicationUserDetailsService service = new ApplicationUserDetailsService(repository); ①
        when(repository.findByEmailIgnoreCase(Users.OFFICER_EMAIL)) ②

.thenReturn(Optional.of(Users.officer()));

        UserDetails userDetails =
service.loadUserByUsername(Users.OFFICER_EMAIL); ③
        assertThat(userDetails).isNotNull();
        assertThat(userDetails.getUsername()).isEqualTo(Users.OFFICER_EMAIL);
④

assertThat(userDetails.getAuthorities()).extracting(GrantedAuthority::getAuthority)
                                                      .contains("ROLE_OFFICER"); ⑤

assertThat(userDetails).isInstanceOfSatisfying(ApplicationUserDetails.class,
⑥
                                                      applicationUserDetails
-> {

assertThat(applicationUserDetails.getUserId())
```

```
        .isEqualTo(Users.officer().getId());
                                                            });
    }

    @Test(expected = UsernameNotFoundException.class) ⑦
    public void givenNotExistingUsername_whenLoadingUser_exceptionThrown() {
        UserRepository repository = mock(UserRepository.class);
        ApplicationUserDetailsService service = new
ApplicationUserDetailsService(repository);

when(repository.findByEmailIgnoreCase(anyString())).thenReturn(Optional.empty
());

        service.loadUserByUsername("i@donotexist.com");
    }
}
```

① You create your object under test, injecting a mock `UserRepository`.

② If a user with email address `Users.OFFICER_EMAIL` is requested to the repository, return the appropriate `User` object.

③ Execute the method.

④ Check the returned object for the appropriate username.

⑤ Check that the granted authorities are what they should be.

⑥ Validate that you return an instance of `ApplicationUserDetails` and that the `userId` property is correct.

⑦ This test tries to find a user that does not exist, so you expect an exception to be thrown.

Since this example uses JUnit with AssertJ, there are two ways to assert that an exception is thrown. You can use the expected attribute on the @Test annotation as done here or you can use assertThatThrownBy from AssertJ. In that case, the code would look like this:

```
@Test
public void
givenNotExistingUsername_whenLoadingUser_exceptionThrown(
) {
    UserRepository repository =
mock(UserRepository.class);
    ApplicationUserDetailsService service = new
ApplicationUserDetailsService(repository);

when(repository.findByEmailIgnoreCase(anyString())).thenR
eturn(Optional.empty());


    assertThatThrownBy(() ->
service.loadUserByUsername("i@donotexist.com"))

.isInstanceOf(UsernameNotFoundException.class);

}
```

Choose whatever you feel is more readable for the test you are writing.

Supporting beans

To get your application up and running, you need two more implementations:

- a `PasswordEncoder` for encoding a user-supplied password into something that can be safely stored in the database, and
- a `TokenStore` for storing generated access and refresh tokens.

Luckily, you don't have to write these yourself. You can use the implementations that Spring provides. To do so, add the following two bean declarations to `CopsbootApplication`:

```
@Bean
public PasswordEncoder passwordEncoder() {
    return new BCryptPasswordEncoder();
}

@Bean
public TokenStore tokenStore() {
    return new InMemoryTokenStore();
}
```

Use the `InMemoryTokenStore` to get started. Later on, you will use the `JdbcTokenStore` to store the tokens in the database.

Test getting an access token

Test using Postman

You're almost ready to test the first piece of your application: try to get an access token from it (although you won't be able to do anything with the token since you have not written a REST controller yet). For this, you just need to wire up a bit more infrastructure.

You need to create a user so you have a username and password to test with. For this purpose, create a `DevelopmentDbInitializer` class that implements the `ApplicationRunner` interface. Spring Boot will run all classes that have this interface after the application starts, a perfect time to add your test user:

REST API Security

```
package com.example.copsboot;

import com.example.copsboot.infrastructure.SpringProfiles;
import com.example.copsboot.user.UserService;
import org.springframework.beans.factory.annotation.Autowired;
import org.springframework.boot.ApplicationArguments;
import org.springframework.boot.ApplicationRunner;
import org.springframework.context.annotation.Profile;
import org.springframework.stereotype.Component;

@Component ①
@Profile(SpringProfiles.DEV) ②
public class DevelopmentDbInitializer implements ApplicationRunner {

    private final UserService userService;

    @Autowired
    public DevelopmentDbInitializer(UserService userService) { ③
        this.userService = userService;
    }

    @Override
    public void run(ApplicationArguments applicationArguments) { ④
        createTestUsers();
    }

    private void createTestUsers() {
        userService.createOfficer("officer@example.com", "officer"); ⑤
    }
}
```

① Mark the class with @Component so the component scanning picks it up.

② The @Profile annotation ensures that this ApplicationRunner only executes if the dev profile is active. See Spring Profiles for more information.

③ Inject the UserService interface, which you will use to create the users.

④ This is the method of the ApplicationRunner interface that you need to implement.

⑤ This is the actual creation of the test user.

> You could also opt to create the test user account using SQL by adding an `import.sql` at the root of the class path. However, it is easier to use Java code to write simple loops to generate a lot of test data, if you want to test pagination for example. On top of that, it is also easier to enable/disable using the Spring Profile.

To support your `DevelopmentDbInitializer`, create a new interface `UserService` with its default implementation `UserServiceImpl`:

UserService.java

```
package com.example.copsboot.user;

public interface UserService {
    User createOfficer(String email, String password);
}
```

UserServiceImpl.java

```
package com.example.copsboot.user;

import org.springframework.beans.factory.annotation.Autowired;
import org.springframework.security.crypto.password.PasswordEncoder;
import org.springframework.stereotype.Service;

@Service
public class UserServiceImpl implements UserService {
    private final UserRepository repository;
    private final PasswordEncoder passwordEncoder;

    @Autowired
    public UserServiceImpl(UserRepository repository, PasswordEncoder passwordEncoder) {
        this.repository = repository;
        this.passwordEncoder = passwordEncoder;
    }

    @Override
    public User createOfficer(String email, String password) {
        User user = User.createOfficer(repository.nextId(), email,
passwordEncoder.encode(password));
        return repository.save(user);
    }
}
```

Now that you have everything in place, you can start your application and

REST API Security

try to get an access token. I like to use Postman [https://www.getpostman.com/] as it has a nice UI and you can use it to store requests for future reference, but you can use any tool you like of course.

Follow these steps in Postman to set up the request:

1. Select POST instead of the default GET.
2. Set the URL to http://localhost:8080/oauth/token.
3. On the Authorization tab, select Basic Auth.

> See "Basic access authentication" on Wikipedia [https://en.wikipedia.org/wiki/Basic_access_authentication] to learn more about that.

4. For username, type copsboot-mobile-client. As password, type ccUyb6vS4S8nxfbKPCrN. See OAuth2ServerConfiguration on where to get those values.
5. Click on Preview Request. This will add the Authorization header to the request.
6. Select the Body tab.
7. Select x-www-form-urlencoded from the radio-button selection.
8. Add the following keys and values:

Key	Value
username	officer@example.com [mailto:officer@example.com]
password	officer
grant_type	password
client_id	copsboot-mobile-client
client_secret	ccUyb6vS4S8nxfbKPCrN

> The client_id and client_secret are in fact optional in the request body since you already used that in the Basic Authentication header. However, if you add them, they need to match the credentials used in the Basic Authentication header.

9. Press "Send".

⚠️ Don't forget to start the application with the dev profile. Otherwise, you will get a 400 BAD REQUEST with the following response:

```
{
    "error": "invalid_grant",
    "error_description": "Bad credentials"
}
```

You can check which profiles are active at startup since Spring Boot prints them:

```
The following profiles are active: dev
```

If all went well, you should get the following JSON response:

```
{
    "access_token": "4329339a-ea9b-4781-86d1-1f49193fa5b3",
    "token_type": "bearer",
    "refresh_token": "90d46c41-9aa0-4c23-88e3-8d4ca4e77b30",
    "expires_in": 43199,
    "scope": "mobile_app"
}
```

REST API Security

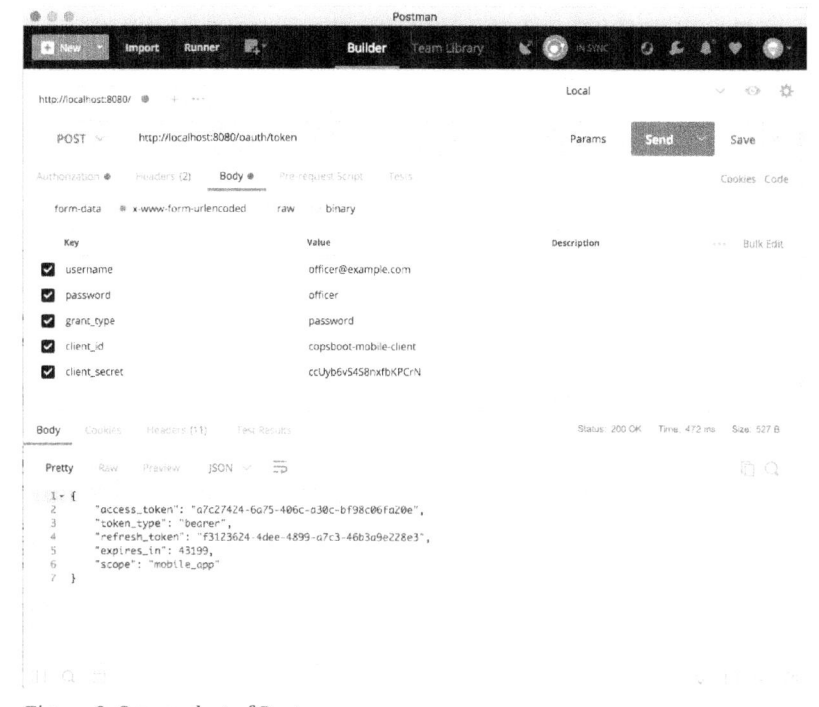

Figure 2. Screenshot of Postman

The response contains an access_token as well as a refresh_token. The access_token is what you need to use in your requests. However, the access_token expires after a configurable amount of time. This is indicated by the expires_in field that returns how many seconds the access_token can still be used. When the access_token expires, the refresh_token can be used to obtain a new access_token without the need for the user's password.

Note that the refresh_token can also expire (or be revoked at the server). In that case, the client application will need to request the user's username and password again to obtain a new access_token and refresh_token from the server.

Unit test to get access token

To ensure your /oauth/token works as expected, write a unit test for it. You will start the whole application and hit the endpoint to see if you get an access token back.

Unit test?

> You might be thinking that unit testing and starting the whole application are not things that really go well together. And you are right. But JUnit is a very capable test framework. It can do so much more than just unit testing, including a full component test, which is what we're doing here.
>
> You will later on see some more techniques for avoiding starting the whole application like you did in the User Repository chapter with `@DataJpaTest`.

Let's take a look at the test:

```
package com.example.copsboot.infrastructure.security;

import com.example.copsboot.infrastructure.SpringProfiles;
import com.example.copsboot.user.UserService;
import com.example.copsboot.user.Users;
import org.junit.Test;
import org.junit.runner.RunWith;
import org.springframework.beans.factory.annotation.Autowired;
import org.springframework.boot.test.autoconfigure.web.servlet.AutoConfigureMockMvc;
import org.springframework.boot.test.context.SpringBootTest;
import org.springframework.test.context.ActiveProfiles;
import org.springframework.test.context.junit4.SpringRunner;
import org.springframework.test.web.servlet.MockMvc;
import org.springframework.util.LinkedMultiValueMap;
import org.springframework.util.MultiValueMap;

import static org.springframework.security.test.web.servlet.request.SecurityMockMvcRequestPostProcessors.httpBasic;
import static org.springframework.test.web.servlet.request.MockMvcRequestBuilders.post;
import static org.springframework.test.web.servlet.result.MockMvcResultHandlers.print;
import static org.springframework.test.web.servlet.result.MockMvcResultMatchers.*;

@RunWith(SpringRunner.class)
@SpringBootTest ①
@AutoConfigureMockMvc ②
@ActiveProfiles(SpringProfiles.TEST)
public class OAuth2ServerConfigurationTest {

    @Autowired
```

REST API Security

```java
    private MockMvc mvc; ③

    @Autowired
    private UserService userService; ④

    @Test
    public void testGetAccessTokenAsOfficer() throws Exception {

        userService.createOfficer(Users.OFFICER_EMAIL,
Users.OFFICER_PASSWORD); ⑤

        String clientId = "copsboot-mobile-client";
        String clientSecret = "ccUyb6vS4S8nxfbKPCrN";

        MultiValueMap<String, String> params = new LinkedMultiValueMap<>();
        params.add("grant_type", "password");
        params.add("client_id", clientId);
        params.add("client_secret", clientSecret);
        params.add("username", Users.OFFICER_EMAIL);
        params.add("password", Users.OFFICER_PASSWORD);

        mvc.perform(post("/oauth/token") ⑥
                            .params(params) ⑦
                            .with(httpBasic(clientId, clientSecret)) ⑧
                            .accept("application/json;charset=UTF-8"))
            .andExpect(status().isOk())
            .andExpect(content().contentType("application/json;charset=UTF-8"))
            .andDo(print()) ⑨
            .andExpect(jsonPath("access_token").isString()) ⑩
            .andExpect(jsonPath("token_type").value("bearer"))
            .andExpect(jsonPath("refresh_token").isString())
            .andExpect(jsonPath("expires_in").isNumber())
            .andExpect(jsonPath("scope").value("mobile_app"))
            ;
    }

}
```

① `@SpringBootTest` indicates that the complete application should be started with a mock servlet environment.

② The mock servlet environment can be automatically configured as you don't require any special configuration for this test.

③ Autowire the `MockMvc` instance so you can test your endpoint.

④ Also autowire `UserService` to create a test user for authentication.

⑤ Create a user for testing. Note that your user from `DevelopmentDbInitializer` is not created here as you are not running with the dev profile.

71

⑥ Perform a HTTP POST on /oauth/token like you did in Postman.

⑦ Add the various parameters like username, password, client_id, etc.

⑧ Add the basic authentication header to authenticate the client application.

⑨ This call will print out the request and response. This is not needed at all for the unit test, but can be quite useful to debug what is going on.

⑩ Use these assertions to see if you get back what you expect.

Refactoring for configurability

While everything now works fine, it feels wrong to have your production client_id and client_secret in your unit test. Luckily, Spring Boot makes externalizing configuration a breeze. You can define a class to hold your own properties and use them like the built-in properties of Spring Boot, like server.port for example. See the Properties chapter if you want to revisit that information.

First, you need to add an extra dependency to Maven's pom.xml:

```
<dependency>
    <groupId>org.springframework.boot</groupId>
    <artifactId>spring-boot-configuration-processor</artifactId>
    <optional>true</optional>
</dependency>
```

This dependency adds an annotation-configuration processor in the build process that adds metadata [https://docs.spring.io/spring-boot/docs/current/reference/html/configuration-metadata.html] about the properties so your IDE might offer coding assistance for them.

After this, create a POJO to hold your two properties:

```
package com.example.copsboot.infrastructure.security;

import org.springframework.boot.context.properties.ConfigurationProperties;
import org.springframework.stereotype.Component;

@Component ①
@ConfigurationProperties(prefix = "copsboot-security") ②
public class SecurityConfiguration {
    private String mobileAppClientId;
    private String mobileAppClientSecret;

    public String getMobileAppClientId() {
        return mobileAppClientId;
    }

    public void setMobileAppClientId(String mobileAppClientId) {
        this.mobileAppClientId = mobileAppClientId;
    }

    public String getMobileAppClientSecret() {
        return mobileAppClientSecret;
    }

    public void setMobileAppClientSecret(String mobileAppClientSecret) {
        this.mobileAppClientSecret = mobileAppClientSecret;
    }
}
```

① @Component creates an instance to autowire later on.

② @ConfigurationProperties indicates to the configuration processor that the properties of this class must be made available for externalized configuration.

Now, you can autowire the SecurityConfiguration into the AuthorizationServerConfiguration inner class of OAuth2ServerConfiguration:

```
@Configuration
@EnableAuthorizationServer
protected static class AuthorizationServerConfiguration extends
AuthorizationServerConfigurerAdapter {

    @Autowired
    private AuthenticationManager authenticationManager;

    @Autowired
    private UserDetailsService userDetailsService;

    @Autowired
    private PasswordEncoder passwordEncoder;

    @Autowired
    private TokenStore tokenStore;

    @Autowired
    private SecurityConfiguration securityConfiguration; ①

    @Override
    public void configure(AuthorizationServerSecurityConfigurer security)
throws Exception {
        security.passwordEncoder(passwordEncoder);
    }

    @Override
    public void configure(ClientDetailsServiceConfigurer clients) throws
Exception {
        clients.inMemory()
                .withClient(securityConfiguration.getMobileAppClientId())
②
                .authorizedGrantTypes("password", "refresh_token")
                .scopes("mobile_app")
                .resourceIds(RESOURCE_ID)

.secret(passwordEncoder.encode(securityConfiguration.getMobileAppClientSecret
())); ③
    }

    @Override
    public void configure(AuthorizationServerEndpointsConfigurer
endpoints) throws Exception {
        endpoints.tokenStore(tokenStore)
                .authenticationManager(authenticationManager)
                .userDetailsService(userDetailsService);
    }
}
```

① Autowire the `SecurityConfiguration` instance.

② Use the client ID from the configuration.

③ Use the client secret from the configuration.

All that is left now is to define the properties using one of the many options Spring Boot has for externalized configuration [https://docs.spring.io/spring-boot/docs/current/reference/html/boot-features-external-config.html]. You want different client IDs and secrets for development, staging, production, and testing, so create application-dev.properties, application-staging.properties, application-prod.properties, and application-test.properties. Since that last one is only needed for unit testing, create it in the src/test/resources folder.

Due to the configuration processor, your IDE can offer coding assistance:

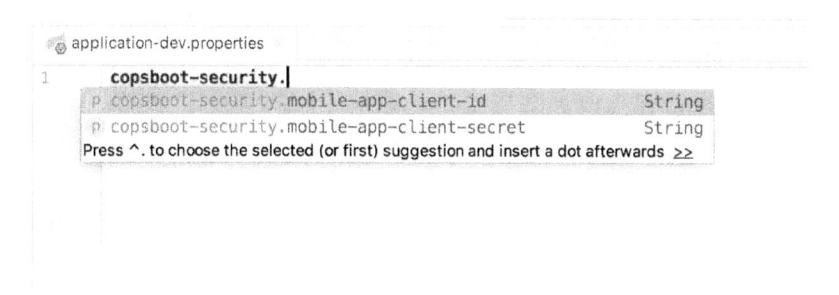

```
application-dev.properties
1       copsboot-security.|
        p copsboot-security.mobile-app-client-id          String
        p copsboot-security.mobile-app-client-secret      String
        Press ^. to choose the selected (or first) suggestion and insert a dot afterwards >>
```

This is application-dev.properties:

```
copsboot-security.mobile-app-client-id=copsboot-mobile-client
copsboot-security.mobile-app-client-secret=ccUyb6vS4S8nxfbKPCrN
```

And this is application-test.properties:

```
copsboot-security.mobile-app-client-id=test-client-id
copsboot-security.mobile-app-client-secret=test-client-secret
```

You can now update your testGetAccessTokenAsOfficer method in OAuth2ServerConfigurationTest to use the values defined in application-test.properties by replacing:

```
String clientId = "copsboot-mobile-client";
String clientSecret = "ccUyb6vS4S8nxfbKPCrN";
```

with:

```
String clientId = "test-client-id";
String clientSecret = "test-client-secret";
```

Note that the `test` profile is active in the test due to the `@ActiveProfiles` annotation at the class level.

Summary

In this chapter, you have added OAuth2 authentication to your application. You also created unit tests for it.

CHAPTER SIX

User REST Controller

Next up in the application is allowing users to create an account via the mobile app. To make this possible, you will add a REST controller.

Basics

Spring Boot allows you to create `Controller` or `RestController` classes to expose the services of your application over HTTP. The main difference between them is that `Controller` is for building server-side generated HTML. It is mostly used with Thymeleaf [https://www.thymeleaf.org/], for example.

`RestController` is what this example will use, since you want to expose JSON over HTTP.

Get mapping

Production code

Start by creating a `UserRestController` class in the `com.example.copsboot.user.web` package. Group all controller-related classes in a `web` package below the functional package (`user` in this example) to keep things cleanly organised.

Add a single route `/api/users/me` to return information on the currently logged-on user. This is nothing spectacular but shows you how a GET mapping works and how to get information on the user that is doing the request.

User REST Controller

```
package com.example.copsboot.user.web;

import com.example.copsboot.infrastructure.security.ApplicationUserDetails;
import com.example.copsboot.user.User;
import com.example.copsboot.user.UserNotFoundException;
import com.example.copsboot.user.UserService;
import org.springframework.beans.factory.annotation.Autowired;
import org.springframework.security.core.annotation.AuthenticationPrincipal;
import org.springframework.web.bind.annotation.GetMapping;
import org.springframework.web.bind.annotation.RequestMapping;
import org.springframework.web.bind.annotation.RestController;

@RestController ①
@RequestMapping("/api/users") ②
public class UserRestController {

    private final UserService service;

    @Autowired
    public UserRestController(UserService service) { ③
        this.service = service;
    }

    @GetMapping("/me") ④
    public UserDto currentUser(@AuthenticationPrincipal ApplicationUserDetails userDetails) { ⑤
        User user = service.getUser(userDetails.getUserId()) ⑥
                           .orElseThrow(() -> new UserNotFoundException(userDetails.getUserId()));
        return UserDto.fromUser(user); ⑦
    }
}
```

① Annotate the class with `RestController` so Spring will pick this class up in component scanning and register the routes for it.

② Set the base route for all methods in this class to /api/user.

③ Autowire the `UserService` since that class will do the actual work.

④ This indicates that this method should be called when a get is done on /me (appended to the base route of the class, so the full path will be /api/users/me).

⑤ Add a parameter of type `ApplicationUserDetails` and annotate it with `@AuthenticationPrincipal` to get information on the user that is doing the request.

⑥ Ask the `UserService` for the user that matches the given ID. Since the service returns an `Optional`, this throws a custom exception `UserNotFoundException` when there is no user with the given ID (which would be quite rare since it is the ID of the currently logged-on user).

⑦ Convert the User entity into a UserDto object for serialization to JSON.

For that @AuthenticationPrincipal, the type of the class has to match with the object returned in the ApplicationUserDetailsService. Otherwise, the object will be null. (You can also set errorOnInvalidType on the annotation to make Spring fail if the type does not match.)

If there is no authenticated user, the parameter might also be null. However, in this case, the route is protected (see OAuth2ServerConfiguration) so this parameter will never be null.

> *Why not return the User entity object?*
>
> It is perfectly possible to return the User object directly in the controller method. The advantage of that is you don't need to create an extra object with fields that closely resemble the entity. However, you most likely want to format the data a bit differently, you want to hide some information, or you want to add extra information from somewhere else.
>
> Changes are so much easier if you directly use a data transfer object (DTO) and avoid annotating your entity with Jackson annotations, which can lead to more annotations than code if you are not careful.

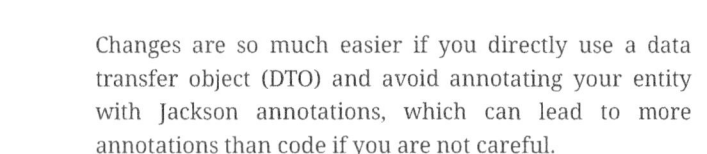

The UserDto object is straightforward:

User REST Controller

```
package com.example.copsboot.user.web;

import com.example.copsboot.user.User;
import com.example.copsboot.user.UserId;
import com.example.copsboot.user.UserRole;
import lombok.Value;

import java.util.Set;

@Value
public class UserDto {
    private final UserId id;
    private final String email;
    private final Set<UserRole> roles;

    public static UserDto fromUser(User user) {
        return new UserDto(user.getId(),
                           user.getEmail(),
                           user.getRoles());
    }
}
```

You notice the fields and a single static factory method to convert from a User entity object to a UserDto. One special thing that is done is the @Value annotation from the Project Lombok [https://projectlombok.org/]. This annotation adds getters for each field and a single constructor for taking each field. It will also generate a proper equals() and hashCode implementation.

To make it work, add the following dependency to your Maven build:

```
<dependency>
    <groupId>org.projectlombok</groupId>
    <artifactId>lombok</artifactId>
</dependency>
```

> Be sure to install the Lombok plugin for your IDE as well so that it is aware of the generated code.
>
> One of the downsides of Lombok is that the IDE must support it, as the code of UserDto is not valid Java without taking into account what the library does.

For completeness, this is the implementation of the UserNotFoundException:

81

```
package com.example.copsboot.user;

import org.springframework.http.HttpStatus;
import org.springframework.web.bind.annotation.ResponseStatus;

@ResponseStatus(HttpStatus.NOT_FOUND) ①
public class UserNotFoundException extends RuntimeException {
    public UserNotFoundException(UserId userId) {
        super(String.format("Could not find user with id %s",
userId.asString()));
    }
}
```

① By annotating the exception with `@ResponseStatus`, Spring will use that status code in the response when this exception gets thrown in a controller.

That is all that there is to it to creating your own REST API. To ensure it works correctly, add a unit test for it, of course.

Testing

To test the functionality, again use Spring Boot's test slicing. This time, use the `@WebMvcTest` annotation to start a mock servlet environment for testing.

UserRestControllerTest.java

```
@RunWith(SpringRunner.class) ①
@WebMvcTest(UserRestController.class) ②
@ActiveProfiles(SpringProfiles.TEST) ③
public class UserRestControllerTest {

    @Autowired
    private MockMvc mvc; ④

    @MockBean
    private UserService service; ⑤
```

① Use the Spring Runner to enable test slicing.

② Use `@WebMvcTest` with a reference to the controller you want to test.

③ Activate the `test` profile.

④ This is the `MockMvc` instance that the testing framework will autowire to drive the mock servlet environment.

⑤ This is the mocked instance of the `UserService` since the controller needs to get it autowired.

User REST Controller

To make your unit test as realistic as possible, ensure that it uses the same security configuration as your actual application. For this purpose, add an inner class for the testing framework to use as the Spring context for the test. Any static inner class that is annotated with `@TestConfiguration` will be picked up when the test runs and the beans defined there will be put in the Spring context together with the automatically created beans from the `@WebMvcTest` annotation.

This is the inner class for this test:

UserRestControllerTest.java

```java
@TestConfiguration ①
@Import(OAuth2ServerConfiguration.class) ②
static class TestConfig {
    @Bean
    public UserDetailsService userDetailsService() {
        return new StubUserDetailsService(); ③
    }

    @Bean
    public TokenStore tokenStore() {
        return new InMemoryTokenStore(); ④
    }

    @Bean
    public SecurityConfiguration securityConfiguration() {
        return new SecurityConfiguration(); ⑤
    }
}
```

① Annotate the inner class with `@TestConfiguration` so the testing framework picks it up.

② Import your actual security configuration from the application.

③ The security configuration needs a `UserDetailsService`. Provide a mock implementation where you know the available users, just for testing.

④ Use the in-memory variant of the TokenStore for testing.

⑤ Use the default `SecurityConfiguration` bean. As you are running with the test profile, this will be filled with the values from application-test.properties.

The `StubUserDetailsService` class looks like this:

```
package com.example.copsboot.infrastructure.security;

import com.example.copsboot.user.Users;
import org.springframework.security.core.userdetails.UserDetails;
import org.springframework.security.core.userdetails.UserDetailsService;
import
org.springframework.security.core.userdetails.UsernameNotFoundException;

public class StubUserDetailsService implements UserDetailsService {

    @Override
    public UserDetails loadUserByUsername(String username) throws
UsernameNotFoundException {
        switch (username) {
            case Users.OFFICER_EMAIL:
                return new ApplicationUserDetails(Users.officer());
            case Users.CAPTAIN_EMAIL:
                return new ApplicationUserDetails(Users.captain());
            default:
                throw new UsernameNotFoundException(username);
        }
    }
}
```

So there are two possible users to authenticate in your unit test.

With this configuration in place, you can write your first test, which is if there is no authorization header, then the application should return a *401 Unauthorized* status code:

```
@Test
public void givenNotAuthenticated_whenAskingMyDetails_forbidden() throws
Exception {
    mvc.perform(get("/api/users/me"))  ①
        .andExpect(status().isUnauthorized());  ②
}
```

① Perform a GET on /api/users/me (the get() is a static import from MockMvcRequestBuilders).

② Validate that you get back a *401 Unauthorized* status code (status() is statically imported from MockMvcResultMatchers).

If you authorize as an officer, you should get back some JSON:

User REST Controller

```
    @Test
    public void
givenAuthenticatedAsOfficer_whenAskingMyDetails_detailsReturned() throws
Exception {
        String accessToken = obtainAccessToken(mvc, Users.OFFICER_EMAIL,
Users.OFFICER_PASSWORD); ①


when(service.getUser(Users.officer().getId())).thenReturn(Optional.of(Users.o
fficer()));  ②

        mvc.perform(get("/api/users/me")  ③
                        .header(HEADER_AUTHORIZATION,
bearer(accessToken)))  ④
            .andExpect(status().isOk())  ⑤
            .andExpect(jsonPath("id").exists())  ⑥
            .andExpect(jsonPath("email").value(Users.OFFICER_EMAIL))
            .andExpect(jsonPath("roles").isArray())
            .andExpect(jsonPath("roles[0]").value("OFFICER"))
        ;
    }
```

① Get an access token using the known email and password of the officer that you also used in `StubUserDetailsService`.

② Set up the `UserService` mock to behave like the actual service would. Given the correct user ID, return the user object.

③ Perform a GET on /api/users/me.

④ Add the authorization header with Bearer <access_token> as value.

⑤ Check if the response status code is *200 Ok*.

⑥ Check the JSON response structure using `MockMvcResultMatchers.jsonPath()`.

To make the test so succinct, you need a helper class, `SecurityHelperForMockMvc`, that can statically import `obtainAccessToken` to get an OAuth2 access token for a given email and password. There is also a constant defined for the `Authorization` header and a `bearer` method to prepend "Bearer" to the access token, as this is required for the `Authorization` header.

This is the full code of this supporting class:

```
package com.example.copsboot.infrastructure.security;

import org.springframework.boot.json.JacksonJsonParser;
import org.springframework.test.web.servlet.MockMvc;
```

85

```java
import org.springframework.test.web.servlet.ResultActions;
import org.springframework.util.LinkedMultiValueMap;
import org.springframework.util.MultiValueMap;

import static
org.springframework.security.test.web.servlet.request.SecurityMockMvcRequestPostProcessors.httpBasic;
import static
org.springframework.test.web.servlet.request.MockMvcRequestBuilders.post;
import static
org.springframework.test.web.servlet.result.MockMvcResultMatchers.content;
import static
org.springframework.test.web.servlet.result.MockMvcResultMatchers.status;

public class SecurityHelperForMockMvc {

    private static final String UNIT_TEST_CLIENT_ID = "test-client-id"; ①
    private static final String UNIT_TEST_CLIENT_SECRET = "test-client-secret"; ②

    public static final String HEADER_AUTHORIZATION = "Authorization";

    /**
     * Allows to get an access token for the given user in the context of a spring (unit) test
     * using MockMVC.
     *
     * @param mvc       the MockMvc instance
     * @param username the username
     * @param password the password
     * @return the <code>access_token</code> to be used in the <code>Authorization</code> header
     * @throws Exception if no token could be obtained.
     */
    public static String obtainAccessToken(MockMvc mvc, String username, String password) throws Exception {

        MultiValueMap<String, String> params = new LinkedMultiValueMap<>();
        params.add("grant_type", "password");
        params.add("client_id", UNIT_TEST_CLIENT_ID);
        params.add("client_secret", UNIT_TEST_CLIENT_SECRET);
        params.add("username", username);
        params.add("password", password);

        ResultActions result
                = mvc.perform(post("/oauth/token")
                                    .params(params)
                                    .with(httpBasic(UNIT_TEST_CLIENT_ID, UNIT_TEST_CLIENT_SECRET))
                                    .accept("application/json;charset=UTF-8"))
                        .andExpect(status().isOk());
```

User REST Controller

```
        .andExpect(content().contentType("application/json;charset=UTF-8"));

        String resultString =
result.andReturn().getResponse().getContentAsString();

        JacksonJsonParser jsonParser = new JacksonJsonParser();
        return
jsonParser.parseMap(resultString).get("access_token").toString();
    }

    public static String bearer(String accessToken) {
        return "Bearer " + accessToken;
    }
}
```

① The client id used for testing. This has to match with the value in application-test.properties.

② The client secret used for testing. This has to match with the value in application-test.properties.

Having started with this simple GET request, take this a step further and do a POST.

POST mapping

You want your mobile-app users to be able to create an account via the REST API. For this purpose, you will expose the /api/users endpoint. This endpoint will accept a JSON body with the parameters needed to create the user account.

To get started, first create a class to hold the parameters:

87

```
package com.example.copsboot.user.web;

import lombok.Data;
import org.hibernate.validator.constraints.Email;

import javax.validation.constraints.NotNull;
import javax.validation.constraints.Size;

@Data
public class CreateOfficerParameters {
    @NotNull
    @Email
    private String email;

    @NotNull
    @Size(min = 6, max = 1000)
    private String password;
}
```

Notice how each field has annotations that are used for validation. Spring will map the received JSON onto the `CreateOfficerParameters` class (using Jackson), but if the validation fails, a *400 Bad Request* will automatically be returned to the client.

We have three annotations here:

- `@NotNull` ensures the field is present in the JSON.
- `@Email` validates the String value as an email address.
- `@Size` validates that the String length falls between the `min` and `max` values.

Now add your endpoint to `UserRestController`:

```
    @PostMapping ①
    @ResponseStatus(HttpStatus.CREATED) ②
    public UserDto createOfficer(@Valid @RequestBody CreateOfficerParameters
parameters) { ③
        User officer = service.createOfficer(parameters.getEmail(), ④
                                             parameters.getPassword());
        return UserDto.fromUser(officer); ⑤
    }
```

① Mark this method to react to a HTTP POST request. As there is no path specified here, it uses the one specified on the class level in the `@RequestMapping("/api/users")` annotation.

User REST Controller

② Upon successful execution of this method, return a status code *201 Created* to the client.

③ @RequestBody tells Spring to deserialize the JSON that gets posted to the CreateOfficerParameters object. The @Valid annotation before that will make Spring validate the parameters object as well.

④ Call the UserService to do the actual work of creating a new user account.

⑤ Return the created user object as a UserDto to the client. This object is in turn serialized by Jackson into a JSON representation.

> The controller should be as lightweight as possible. All the actual logic should be done in a service class, and the controller should only be concerned with HTTP concerns like serialization, validation, etc....

Now add a new test case in UserRestControllerTest to ensure all is well:

```
@Test
public void testCreateOfficer() throws Exception {
    String email = "wim.deblauwe@example.com";
    String password = "my-super-secret-pwd";

    CreateOfficerParameters parameters = new CreateOfficerParameters();
    parameters.setEmail(email);
    parameters.setPassword(password);

    when(service.createOfficer(email,
password)).thenReturn(Users.newOfficer(email, password));  ①

    mvc.perform(post("/api/users")  ②
                    .contentType(MediaType.APPLICATION_JSON_UTF8)  ③
.content(objectMapper.writeValueAsString(parameters)))  ④
            .andExpect(status().isCreated())  ⑤
            .andExpect(jsonPath("id").exists())  ⑥
            .andExpect(jsonPath("email").value(email))
            .andExpect(jsonPath("roles").isArray())
            .andExpect(jsonPath("roles[0]").value("OFFICER"));

    verify(service).createOfficer(email, password);  ⑦
}
```

① Instruct the mock UserService to return a new User object when the createOfficer method is called, just like the actual UserService would do.

② Perform a POST request on /api/users.

③ Set the Content-Type header to indicate that you are going to send JSON.

④ Use the Jackson objectMapper to turn the CreateOfficerParameters object into JSON and use it as the body of the request.

⑤ Check if the response status is *201 Created*.

⑥ Check if the response JSON has the proper fields using jsonPath.

⑦ Verify that the UserService has been called with the correct arguments.

To support your test method, you need to add two extra fields in the class:

```
@Autowired
private ObjectMapper objectMapper; ①
@MockBean
private UserService service; ②
```

① Jackson's ObjectMapper handles conversion from and to JSON. You can autowire this as the testing infrastructure creates an instance for you.

② The controller needs an instance of UserService. You can use @MockBean to ask Mockito to automatically create a mock object so you can verify if certain methods are called on the service when an endpoint is hit.

If you now try to run the test, you will notice that it fails with the following problem:

```
java.lang.AssertionError: Status
Expected :201
Actual   :401
```

You get *401 Unauthorized* instead of the expected *201 Created*. This is normal as your security configuration requires that all calls below /api need to be authenticated. As a "create user" call cannot be authenticated (you have no account to authenticate with yet, of course), you need to change the configuration as follows:

OAuth2ServerConfiguration.java

```
@Override
public void configure(HttpSecurity http) throws Exception {

    http.authorizeRequests()
        .antMatchers(HttpMethod.OPTIONS, "/api/**").permitAll()
        .and()
        .antMatcher("/api/**")
        .authorizeRequests()
        .antMatchers(HttpMethod.POST, "/api/users").permitAll() ①
        .anyRequest().authenticated();
}
```

① Allow anybody to do a POST on /api/users.

Running the test now will result in a green bar.

Writing API documentation

You now have two API endpoints and need to provide documentation so that clients that want to use these endpoints know what to expect from your API. There are various options for documentation (e.g., Swagger [https://swagger.io/] or Postman [https://www.getpostman.com/docs/v6/postman_for_publishers/public_api_docs]) but I really like what Spring REST Docs [https://projects.spring.io/spring-restdocs/] offers in this regard.

Spring REST Docs allows you to generate AsciiDoc [http://asciidoc.org/]-formatted snippets that you can include in documentation you write in Asciidoctor [http://asciidoctor.org/]. You can generate these snippets by running unit tests with Spring MVC Test [https://docs.spring.io/spring/docs/current/spring-framework-reference/htmlsingle#spring-mvc-test-framework].

Your documentation is always up to date, since the JSON in the documentation is the actual JSON that your code produces. You can explain the API in your documentation and include those current JSON snippets as part of the final HTML or PDF document.

Maven setup

The first thing you need to add is the `spring-restdocs-mockmvc` dependency so that you can write unit tests using Mock MVC to generate the JSON snippets:

91

```xml
<dependency>
    <groupId>org.springframework.restdocs</groupId>
    <artifactId>spring-restdocs-mockmvc</artifactId>
    <scope>test</scope>
</dependency>
```

To set up the HTML and PDF output generation, you need to configure the `asciidoctor-maven-plugin` (you can leave out one or the other if you want only HTML or only PDF output):

```xml
<build>
    <pluginManagement>
        <plugins>
            <plugin>
                <groupId>org.asciidoctor</groupId>
                <artifactId>asciidoctor-maven-plugin</artifactId>
                <version>${asciidoctor-maven-plugin.version}</version>
                <dependencies>
                    <dependency>
                        <groupId>org.asciidoctor</groupId>
                        <artifactId>asciidoctorj-pdf</artifactId>
                        <version>1.5.0-alpha.16</version>
                    </dependency>
                    <dependency>
                        <groupId>org.asciidoctor</groupId>
                        <artifactId>asciidoctorj</artifactId>
                        <version>1.5.7</version>
                    </dependency>
                    <dependency>
                        <groupId>org.springframework.restdocs</groupId>
                        <artifactId>spring-restdocs-asciidoctor</artifactId>
                        <version>${spring-restdocs.version}</version>
                    </dependency>
                    <dependency>
                        <groupId>org.jruby</groupId>
                        <artifactId>jruby-complete</artifactId>
                        <version>9.1.17.0</version>
                    </dependency>
                </dependencies>
                <executions>
                    <execution>
                        <id>generate-docs</id>
                        <phase>prepare-package</phase>
                        <goals>
                            <goal>process-asciidoc</goal>
                        </goals>
                        <configuration>
                            <backend>html</backend>
                        </configuration>
                    </execution>
```

```xml
            <execution>
                <id>generate-docs-pdf</id>
                <phase>prepare-package</phase>
                <goals>
                    <goal>process-asciidoc</goal>
                </goals>
                <configuration>
                    <backend>pdf</backend>
                </configuration>
            </execution>
        </executions>
        <configuration>
            <backend>html</backend>
            <doctype>book</doctype>
            <attributes>
                <project-version>${project.version}</project-version>
            </attributes>
        </configuration>
    </plugin>
  </plugins>
</pluginManagement>
```

You are adding this in the `pluginManagement` section of Maven, and the plugin is yet active. This is deliberate as you only want to generate the documentation when running with a certain Maven profile. In this case, I am calling this profile `ci`, as it will be run on our continuous-integration server:

```xml
<profiles>
    <profile>
        <id>ci</id>
        <build>
            <plugins>
                <plugin>
                    <groupId>org.asciidoctor</groupId>
                    <artifactId>asciidoctor-maven-plugin</artifactId>
                    <version>${asciidoctor-maven-plugin.version}</version>
                    <executions>
                        <execution>
                            <id>generate-docs</id>
                            <phase>prepare-package</phase>
                            <goals>
                                <goal>process-asciidoc</goal>
                            </goals>
                        </execution>
                    </executions>
                </plugin>
            </plugins>
        </build>
    </profile>
</profiles>
```

By binding the `process-asciidoc` goal to the `prepare-package`, you ensure that the documentation is built whenever somebody runs `mvn package -Pci` (-P allows you to activate a Maven profile via the command line).

The last step is adding the version-number properties for `asciidoctor-maven-plugin.version` and `spring-restdocs.version`:

```xml
<properties>
    <project.build.sourceEncoding>UTF-8</project.build.sourceEncoding>
    <project.reporting.outputEncoding>UTF-8</project.reporting.outputEncoding>
    <java.version>1.8</java.version>

    <!-- Maven Plugin versions -->
    <asciidoctor-maven-plugin.version>1.5.6</asciidoctor-maven-plugin.version>

    <!-- Project dependencies versions -->
    <guava.version>25.1-jre</guava.version>

    <!-- Test dependencies versions -->
    <spring-restdocs.version>2.0.1.RELEASE</spring-restdocs.version>
</properties>
```

It might seem that using a Maven profile just to generate documentation is a bit of overkill at this point, but you are doing this now to prepare for including more build steps that should only be done on the build server like code coverage and static code analysis.

Asciidoctor document

The Maven setup now allows you to create HTML and PDF output but of course you need a source file. To get started, create `Copsboot REST API Guide.adoc` in the `src/main/asciidoc` folder:

Copsboot REST API Guide.adoc

```
= Copsboot REST API Guide
:icons: font
:toc:
:toclevels: 2

:numbered:

== Introduction

The Copsboot project uses a REST API for interfacing with the server.

This documentation covers version {project-version} of the application.
```

Don't worry about the AsciiDoc syntax for now. If you want, you can read the AsciiDoc Syntax Quick Reference [https://asciidoctor.org/docs/asciidoc-syntax-quick-reference/] or the Asciidoctor User Manual [http://asciidoctor.org/docs/user-manual/] for more information.

Notice how you have `{project-version}` in the source document. If you now run `mvn package -Pci` on the command line, you will get the HTML and PDF output in the `target/generated-docs` folder. There, `{project-version}` is replaced with `0.0.1-SNAPSHOT`, which is the current version of your Maven project.

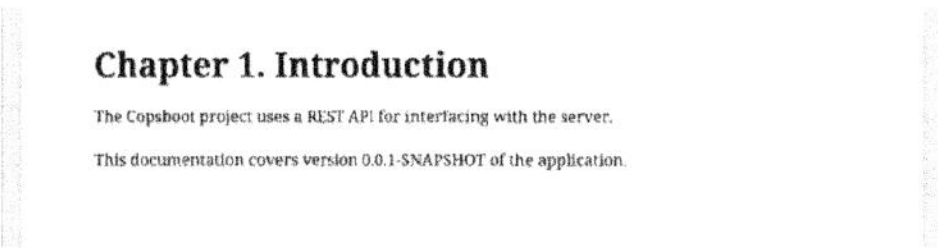

Chapter 1. Introduction

The Copsboot project uses a REST API for interfacing with the server.

This documentation covers version 0.0.1-SNAPSHOT of the application.

Figure 3. Copsboot REST API Guide.pdf

This works because you have made the Maven project version available to

Asciidoctor in the Maven configuration of the plugin:

```
<attributes>
    <project-version>${project.version}</project-version>
</attributes>
```

The name of the XML element is the name of the variable to be used in the Asciidoctor document. The text inside the element is the value, for which this example uses the built-in Maven variable project.version.

This ensures that you always know what version of the software the documentation refers to.

UserRestController documentation

With all of that out of the way, you can create the unit test that will generate the JSON snippets for your documentation. First, create a test class called UserRestControllerDocumentation. The class annotations and the fields you have are almost the same as those you already have in UserRestControllerTest.

UserRestControllerDocumentation.java

```
@RunWith(SpringRunner.class)
@WebMvcTest(UserRestController.class)
@ActiveProfiles(SpringProfiles.TEST)
public class UserRestControllerDocumentation {
    @Rule
    public final JUnitRestDocumentation restDocumentation = new JUnitRestDocumentation("target/generated-snippets");

    private MockMvc mvc;

    @Autowired
    private ObjectMapper objectMapper;
    @MockBean
    private UserService service;
```

There are two differences between this and UserRestControllerTest:

1. The JUnit rule, JUnitRestDocumentation, generates the code snippets and needs to know where to put them. The path here is the default if you are using Maven.

2. The MockMvc field is no longer annotated with @Autowired as you will build the proper instance on which you can apply your own security

User REST Controller

and documentation concerns.

In the `setUp` method of the class, define how you want to generate the snippets:

UserRestControllerDocumentation.java

```
    @Autowired
    private WebApplicationContext context;   ①
    private RestDocumentationResultHandler resultHandler;   ②

    @Before
    public void setUp() {
        resultHandler = document("{method-name}",   ③
                                 preprocessRequest(prettyPrint()),   ④
                                 preprocessResponse(prettyPrint(),   ⑤
  removeMatchingHeaders("X.*",   ⑥

  "Pragma",

  "Expires")));
        mvc = MockMvcBuilders.webAppContextSetup(context)   ⑦
                             .apply(springSecurity())   ⑧

  .apply(documentationConfiguration(restDocumentation))   ⑨
                             .alwaysDo(resultHandler)   ⑩
                             .build();
    }
```

① Ask Spring to autowire the `WebApplicationContext` as you need to this build your `MockMvc` instance.

② This is a reference to `RestDocumentationResultHandler`, for which you will need to add documentation information in the unit tests themselves

③ Build the `resultHandler` reference. Use the unit-test method to name the directory where the snippets will be generated (relative to the directory already specified by the `JUnitRestDocumentation` rule.

④ To ensure the JSON in the documentation looks nice, preprocess all request bodies to pretty-print them.

⑤ Pretty-print the response body too.

⑥ In addition to using pretty printing, remove some of the headers of the response as you don't want them in your documentation.

⑦ Using the `webAppContextSetup` factory method from `MockMvcBuilders`, build your `MockMvc` instance.

97

⑧ Ensure that the MockMvc instance is aware of Spring Security.

⑨ Apply the JUnit rule.

⑩ Ensure the documentation is always generated.

Finally, you need to add the inner class to define the application context of the test:

UserRestControllerDocumentation.java

```
@TestConfiguration
@Import(OAuth2ServerConfiguration.class)
static class TestConfig {
    @Bean
    public UserDetailsService userDetailsService() {
        return new StubUserDetailsService();
    }

    @Bean
    public TokenStore tokenStore() {
        return new InMemoryTokenStore();
    }

    @Bean
    public SecurityConfiguration securityConfiguration() {
        return new SecurityConfiguration();
    }
}
```

Documentation of GET

With this in place, you can write your first documentation test:

UserRestControllerDocumentation.java

```
@Test
public void ownUserDetailsWhenNotLoggedInExample() throws Exception {
    mvc.perform(get("/api/users/me"))
        .andExpect(status().isUnauthorized());
}
```

This basically is just a simple unit test. The only difference is that you import org.springframework.restdocs.mockmvc.RestDocumentationRequestBuilders.get instead of org.springframework.test.web.servlet.request.MockMvcRequestBuilders.get.

User REST Controller

Try running this test. It should generate a directory called own-user-details-when-not-logged-in-example in target/generated-snippets with six files inside it:

- curl-request.adoc,
- http-request.adoc,
- http-response.adoc,
- httpie-request.adoc,
- request-body.adoc, and
- response-body.adoc.

The most important file for your current test is http-response.adoc as this shows the failure response to be expected when calling /api/users/me if you are not authenticated:

```
[source,http,options="nowrap"]
----
HTTP/1.1 401 Unauthorized
Cache-Control: no-cache, no-store, max-age=0, must-revalidate
Cache-Control: no-store
WWW-Authenticate: Bearer realm="copsboot-service", error="unauthorized",
error_description="Full authentication is required to access this resource"
Content-Type: application/json;charset=UTF-8
Content-Length: 113

{
  "error" : "unauthorized",
  "error_description" : "Full authentication is required to access this resource"
}
----
```

You can now include this snippet of Asciidoctor in your API documentation. To split the documentation into small pieces, create the _users.adoc file with this content:

_users.adoc

```
== User Management

=== User information

The API allows to get information on the currently logged on user
via a `GET` on `/api/users/me`. If you are not a logged on user, the
following response will be returned:

operation::own-user-details-when-not-logged-in-example[snippets='http-
request,http-response']
```

Notice the operation:: line at the end of your document. It has two important parts:

1. The part between the :: and the [(own-user-details-when-not-logged-in-example in this example) needs to match the name of the generated directory in the target/generated-snippets folder.

2. The snippets='curl-request,http-response' part defines which of the files in the folder should be included in your documentation. The names match the file names, minus the .adoc extension.

> Start the include file's name with an underscore (_) so that the AsciiDoc Maven plugin will not try to create a separate output file for the include file.

This results in the following PDF after running mvn clean package -Pci:

2.1. User information

The API allows to get information on the currently logged on user via a GET on /api/users/me. If you are not a logged on user, the following response will be returned:

HTTP request

```
GET /api/users/me HTTP/1.1
Host: localhost:8080
```

HTTP response

```
HTTP/1.1 401 Unauthorized
Cache-Control: no-cache, no-store, max-age=0, must-revalidate
Cache-Control: no-store
WWW-Authenticate: Bearer realm="copsboot-service", error="unauthorized",
error_description="Full authentication is required to access this resource"
Content-Type: application/json;charset=UTF-8
Content-Length: 113

{
  "error" : "unauthorized",
  "error_description" : "Full authentication is required to access this resource"
}
```

Documentation of GET with response fields

Your first documentation test could remain simple because you did not need to document the JSON response. The *401 Unauthorized* status code was the most important part.

Now, expand your documentation with a case that involves response fields. Here is a test for an authenticated user with the OFFICER role:

UserRestControllerDocumentation.java

```
    @Test
    public void authenticatedOfficerDetailsExample() throws Exception {
        String accessToken = obtainAccessToken(mvc, Users.OFFICER_EMAIL,
Users.OFFICER_PASSWORD);

when(service.getUser(Users.officer().getId())).thenReturn(Optional.of(Users.o
fficer()));

        mvc.perform(get("/api/users/me")
                        .header(HEADER_AUTHORIZATION,
bearer(accessToken)))
            .andExpect(status().isOk())
            .andDo(resultHandler.document(
                    responseFields(
                            fieldWithPath("id")
                                    .description("The unique id of the
user."),
                            fieldWithPath("email")
                                    .description("The email address of the
user."),
                            fieldWithPath("roles")
                                    .description("The security roles of the
user."))));
    }
```

Using the static methods `responseFields` and `fieldWithPath`, document the reponse fields in the response body. Using `fieldWithPath` not only instructs Spring REST Docs to output a table with the name and description of each field, but also *checks* if the fields are really present in the returned JSON. Spring REST Docs will also fail the unit test if there are fields in the response that are not documented.

In fact, when you run the test now, it fails:

```
org.springframework.restdocs.snippet.SnippetException: The following parts of
the payload were not documented:
{
  "id" : {
    "id" : "02c22858-2e85-4279-85db-3912ae05ca63"
  }
}
```

The problem is that the JSON is generated from `UserDto` where `id` is of type `UserId`, resulting in the nested `id` fields. Luckily, you can easily fix this with Spring Boot by creating a `@JsonComponent` annotated bean:

User REST Controller

com.example.copsboot.infrastructure.json.EntityIdJsonSerializer

```
package com.example.copsboot.infrastructure.json;

import com.example.orm.jpa.EntityId;
import com.fasterxml.jackson.core.JsonGenerator;
import com.fasterxml.jackson.databind.JsonSerializer;
import com.fasterxml.jackson.databind.SerializerProvider;
import org.springframework.boot.jackson.JsonComponent;

import java.io.IOException;

@JsonComponent ①
public class EntityIdJsonSerializer extends JsonSerializer<EntityId> { ②

    @Override
    public void serialize(EntityId entityId, JsonGenerator jsonGenerator,
SerializerProvider serializerProvider) throws IOException {
        jsonGenerator.writeString(entityId.asString()); ③
    }

}
```

① The `@JsonComponent` will force Spring Boot's component scanning to pick up the bean and register it with Jackson.

② Extend from `com.fasterxml.jackson.databind.JsonSerializer` since you want to influence only the serialization process (and not the deserialization).

③ Write the string representation of the entity ID into the JSON (not creating a nested `id` like Jackson does by default).

With this added, the test succeeds and generates a new snippet called `response-fields.adoc`, which looks like this:

```
|===
|Path|Type|Description

|`id`
|`String`
|The unique id of the user.

|`email`
|`String`
|The email address of the user

|`roles`
|`Array`
|The security roles of the user

|===
```

This is an AsciiDoc table to which you can add to your _users.doc. You can for example add something like this:

```
If you do log on as a user, you get more information on that user:

operation::authenticated-officer-details-example[snippets='http-request,http-response,response-fields']
```

Note how we added response-fields as third item in the snippets parameter. This results in the following output (with a HTML example for a change):

User REST Controller

If you do log on as a user, you get more information on that user:

HTTP request

```
GET /api/users/me HTTP/1.1
Authorization: Bearer 31168125-7fc8-4bd6-b8c9-196ebbe699fc
Host: localhost:8080
```

HTTP response

```
HTTP/1.1 200 OK
Cache-Control: no-cache, no-store, max-age=0, must-revalidate
Content-Type: application/json;charset=UTF-8
Content-Length: 113

{
  "id" : "422d0735-9dd8-4710-8e3b-dd047ce62ffe",
  "email" : "officer@example.com",
  "roles" : [ "OFFICER" ]
}
```

Response fields

Path	Type	Description
id	String	The unique id of the user.
email	String	The email address of the user
roles	Array	The security roles of the user

Figure 4. Copsboot REST API Guide.html

Documentation of POST with response fields

As a final example of writing documentation for a REST API, you will document the POST call to create a new user account. Remember, this is how the `UserRestController` defines the POST method:

UserRestController.java

```
    @PostMapping ①
    @ResponseStatus(HttpStatus.CREATED) ②
    public UserDto createOfficer(@Valid @RequestBody CreateOfficerParameters parameters) { ③
        User officer = service.createOfficer(parameters.getEmail(), ④
                                             parameters.getPassword());
        return UserDto.fromUser(officer); ⑤
    }
```

In this case, you need to document the request body as well as the response body. The test method that will generate the documentation snippets looks like this:

105

UserRestControllerDocumentation.java

```
    @Test
    public void createOfficerExample() throws Exception {
        String email = "wim.deblauwe@example.com";
        String password = "my-super-secret-pwd";

        CreateOfficerParameters parameters = new CreateOfficerParameters();   ①
        parameters.setEmail(email);
        parameters.setPassword(password);

        when(service.createOfficer(email,
 password)).thenReturn(Users.newOfficer(email, password));   ②

        mvc.perform(post("/api/users")   ③
                        .contentType(MediaType.APPLICATION_JSON_UTF8)
 .content(objectMapper.writeValueAsString(parameters)))   ④
                .andExpect(status().isCreated())   ⑤
                .andDo(resultHandler.document(
                        requestFields(   ⑥
                                fieldWithPath("email")
                                        .description("The email address of the user to be created."),
                                fieldWithPath("password")
                                        .description("The password for the new user.")
                        ),
                        responseFields(   ⑦
                                fieldWithPath("id")
                                        .description("The unique id of the user."),
                                fieldWithPath("email")
                                        .description("The email address of the user."),
                                fieldWithPath("roles")
                                        .description("The security roles of the user."))));
    }
```

① Create the request body object that will be serialized to JSON.

② Set up the mock `UserService` to behave as the real service would.

③ Execute a POST on /api/users.

④ Serialze the `CreateOfficerParameters` to JSON using Jackson's `ObjectMapper`.

⑤ This sanity check ensures that you get the proper response status code.

⑥ Document the request body using `fieldWithPath` static methods.

User REST Controller

⑦ Document the response body as you did in Documentation of GET with response fields.

With this test in place, update your `_user.adoc` documentation file again:

_users.adoc

```
=== Create a user

To create an new user, do a `POST` on `/api/users`:

operation::create-officer-example[snippets='http-request,request-fields,http-response,response-fields']
```

Note how you added `request-fields` to the snippets parameter.

The resulting PDF looks like this:

2.2. Create a user

To create an new user, do a POST on /api/users:

HTTP request

```
POST /api/users HTTP/1.1
Content-Type: application/json;charset=UTF-8
Host: localhost:8080
Content-Length: 80

{
  "email" : "wim.deblauwe@example.com",
  "password" : "my-super-secret-pwd"
}
```

Request fields

Path	Type	Description
email	String	The email address of the user to be created.
password	String	The password for the new user.

HTTP response

If you'd like to add more text in your documentation for each of the snippets, you can include individual snippets one by one by using the include macro instead of the operation macro.

For example:

```
The request fields for the create user call are
documented in this table:

include::{snippets}/create-officer-example/request-
fields.adoc[]
```

To make this work, you need to define the snippets variable in Maven as follows:

```
<plugin>
    <groupId>org.asciidoctor</groupId>
    <artifactId>asciidoctor-maven-plugin</artifactId>
    ...
    <configuration>
        <backend>html</backend>
        <doctype>book</doctype>
        <attributes>
            <snippets>${snippetsDirectory}</snippets>   ①
            <project-version>${project.version}</project-version>
        </attributes>
    </configuration>
```

① Define the snippets variable.

${snippetsDirectory} is a Maven variable that is defined in the <properties/> section of the pom.xml:

```
<properties>
    ...
<snippetsDirectory>${project.build.directory}/generated-snippets</snippetsDirectory>
</properties>
```

Refactoring to avoid duplication

So far, you have built a unit test and some nice documentation for your RestController. However, there is some duplication that you should avoid before it gets out of hand:

- Both `UserRestControllerTest` and `UserRestControllerDocumentation` define that the test profile as active (via `@ActiveProfiles(SpringProfiles.TEST)`).
- Both have the exact same inner class to define the Spring context that should be active during the test.

If you were to create other unit tests and documentation tests for other controllers, you would also duplicate all that there. Luckily, Spring supports meta-annotations [https://docs.spring.io/spring/docs/current/spring-framework-reference/core.html#beans-meta-annotations] so that you can compose your own annotation with defaults like you want them.

The first step is creating your own annotation:

```
@Retention(RetentionPolicy.RUNTIME) ①
@WebMvcTest ②
@ContextConfiguration(classes = CopsbootControllerTestConfiguration.class) ③
@ActiveProfiles(SpringProfiles.TEST) ④
public @interface CopsbootControllerTest {

    @AliasFor(annotation = WebMvcTest.class, attribute = "value") ⑤
    Class<?>[] value() default {};

    @AliasFor(annotation = WebMvcTest.class, attribute = "controllers") ⑥
    Class<?>[] controllers() default {};
}
```

① Set the retention of the annotation to RUNTIME so that Spring can "view" the annotation.

② Add `@WebMvcTest` so that your own annotation gets all the magic of that annotation as well.

③ Define that `CopsbootControllerTestConfiguration` should be the default Spring context that will be loaded.

④ Activate the test profile by default.

⑤ Allow the user of your annotation to pass in the controller under test and pass it in your turn to `@WebMvcTest`.

⑥ Allow the user of your annotation to also use controllers as parameter (next to value as they are just aliases of each other).

The CopsbootControllerTestConfiguration that is loaded by default via the annotation is the inner class from UserControllerTest extracted into a top-level class:

```
package com.example.copsboot.infrastructure.test;

import com.example.copsboot.infrastructure.security.OAuth2ServerConfiguration;
import com.example.copsboot.infrastructure.security.SecurityConfiguration;
import com.example.copsboot.infrastructure.security.StubUserDetailsService;
import org.springframework.boot.test.context.TestConfiguration;
import org.springframework.context.annotation.Bean;
import org.springframework.context.annotation.Import;
import org.springframework.security.core.userdetails.UserDetailsService;
import org.springframework.security.oauth2.provider.token.TokenStore;
import org.springframework.security.oauth2.provider.token.store.InMemoryTokenStore;

@TestConfiguration
@Import(OAuth2ServerConfiguration.class)
public class CopsbootControllerTestConfiguration {
    @Bean
    public UserDetailsService userDetailsService() {
        return new StubUserDetailsService();
    }

    @Bean
    public TokenStore tokenStore() {
        return new InMemoryTokenStore();
    }

    @Bean
    public SecurityConfiguration securityConfiguration() {
        return new SecurityConfiguration();
    }

}
```

You can now update your UserControllerTest from:

```
@RunWith(SpringRunner.class)
@WebMvcTest(UserRestController.class)
@ActiveProfiles(SpringProfiles.TEST)
public class UserRestControllerTest {
```

to:

```
@RunWith(SpringRunner.class)
@CopsbootControllerTest(UserRestController.class)
public class UserRestControllerTest {
```

Additionally, your new `UserRestControllerTest` no longer needs the inner class at the bottom!

In the same way, you can update `UserRestControllerDocumentation` to:

```
@RunWith(SpringRunner.class)
@CopsbootControllerTest(UserRestController.class)
public class UserRestControllerDocumentation {
```

Summary

You have seen how to add GET and POST endpoints to your application and how to map the JSON that is sent to a Java class for further processing in your application.

You have written unit tests and documentation for those endpoints.

This concludes your first encounter with the REST API. It's time to focus on getting a "real" database working.

CHAPTER SEVEN

Working with a Real Database

So far, you have been developing with H2, an in-memory database. If you want to take your application to production, you need to use a "real" database like MySQL, PostgreSQL, or Microsoft SQL Server.

> For the sake of this article, we're assuming that the database is relational and not a NoSQL database, although Spring Data supports many NoSQL databases.

For this example, we will use PostgreSQL [https://www.postgresql.org/], an open-source database, as it is free to use and runs on all major operating systems. It also natively supports UUID columns, which is why I like it over MySQL.

Installation of PostgreSQL

It's easy to install PostgreSQL through Docker so let's do that. Using the official Postgres Docker repository [https://hub.docker.com/_/postgres/], you can install it as follows:

1. Run `docker pull postgres:10.3`.
2. Run `docker run -e 'POSTGRES_PASSWORD=my-postgres-db-pwd' -p 5432:5432 --name my-postgres-db -d postgres:10.3`.
    - Replace `my-postgres-db-pwd` with your password of choice.
    - You can also change `my-postgres-db` to any name you like to use.
3. Running `docker ps` should show that the container is running:

```
Wims-MacBook-Pro:~ wdb$ docker ps
CONTAINER ID     IMAGE            COMMAND                  CREATED
STATUS           PORTS            NAMES
b8e872a7f117     postgres:10.3    "docker-entrypoint.s…"   4
seconds ago      Up 5 seconds     0.0.0.0:5432->5432/tcp   my-
postgres-db
```

That is basically all there is to it. If you want to access the database via command line, you can do this via `docker exec -it my-postgres-db bash`.

This command brings you into the Docker container that runs PostgreSQL. You can now start the client with `psql -U postgres`.

Here, you can create the database: `CREATE DATABASE copsbootdb;`.

Exit from the PostgreSQL client: \q.

And exit from the Docker container: exit.

Using PostgreSQL

Starting up with the local PostgreSQL

The best way to select which database to connect to is with Spring Profiles. You will be using a profile that you'll call local for the connection to your location database. The first thing you need to do is create an application-local.properties file to hold your connection details.

application-local.properties

```
copsboot-security.mobile-app-client-id=copsboot-mobile-client
copsboot-security.mobile-app-client-secret=ccUyb6vS4S8nxfbKPCrN

spring.datasource.url=jdbc:postgresql://localhost/copsbootdb  ①
spring.datasource.driverClassName=org.postgresql.Driver  ②
spring.datasource.username=postgres  ③
spring.datasource.password=my-postgres-db-pwd  ④
spring.jpa.database-platform=org.hibernate.dialect.PostgreSQLDialect  ⑤
spring.jpa.hibernate.ddl-auto=none  ⑥
```

① The JDBC URL defines the kind of database (postgresql), where it is running (localhost), and the name of the database (copsbootdb).

② This is the JDBC driver to use.

③ This is the user that has the appropriate rights on the database.

④ This is the password of the user.

⑤ This is the dialect that our JPA implementation (in our case, Hibernate) should use

⑥ Disable the automatic creation of the database tables by setting this property to none.

115

> This file should never be added to version control as it contains your personal setup and password. A good practise is committing a application-local.properties.template so there is a sample file to start from.
>
> If you are using git, create a .gitignore file and add application-local.properties to it like this:

```
/src/main/resources/application-local.properties
```

Next, you need to update your pom.xml to include the PostgreSQL driver:

```
<dependency>
    <groupId>org.postgresql</groupId>
    <artifactId>postgresql</artifactId>
</dependency>
```

Database table creation

If you now start the application and try to create a user, you would get errors that tell you that you have no tables in your database. With PostgreSQL, this message looks like this:

```
org.postgresql.util.PSQLException: ERROR: relation "copsboot_user" does not exist
```

Spring Boot supports two libraries that allow SQL scripts to run automatically at startup to ensure that your database is up to date: Flyway [https://flywaydb.org/] and Liquibase [https://www.liquibase.org/].

The biggest difference between the two is that Flyways uses SQL scripts while Liquibase uses XML syntax. This project will use Flyway but Liquibase is an equally valid choice. JHipster [https://www.jhipster.tech/] for example uses Liquibase.

Start by adding the dependency in the pom.xml:

Working with a Real Database

```
<dependency>
    <groupId>org.flywaydb</groupId>
    <artifactId>flyway-core</artifactId>
</dependency>
```

Now, create a db/migration directory inside src/main/resources as this is the default location for Flyway.

Inside that directory, create one directory for H2 and one for PostgreSQL that will contain the actual migration scripts. The directory tree will look like this:

```
pom.xml
mvnw
mvnw.cmd
src
  |-- main
       |-- java
            |-- com.springbook.application
                 |-- Application
       |-- resources
            |-- application.properties
            |-- db
                 |-- migration
                      |-- h2
                           |-- V1.0.0.1__authentication.sql ①
                      |-- postgresql
                           |-- V1.0.0.1__authentication.sql ②
                           |-- V1.0.0.2__users.sql ③
  |-- test
       |-- java
            |-- com.springbook.application
                 |-- ApplicationTests
```

① This is the migration script to create the OAuth related tables for H2.

② This is the migration script to create the OAuth related tables for PostgreSQL.

③ This is the migration script to create the copsboot_user table for PostgreSQL.

> The H2 directory only has the script to create the tables for OAuth. All other tables will be created by Hibernate automatically when we run on H2 (by using the dev or test profile).

The name of the script itself is important as Flyway will use that to determine the order in which the scripts are run. See Naming [https://flywaydb.org/documentation/migrations#naming] at the Flyway site for more on that.

Generate DDL scripts

You can manually write those SQL scripts for Flyway, but you can also get a little help from Spring Boot.

Add the following properties to `application-local.properties`:

```
spring.jpa.properties.javax.persistence.schema-generation.create-source=metadata
spring.jpa.properties.javax.persistence.schema-generation.scripts.action=create
spring.jpa.properties.javax.persistence.schema-generation.scripts.create-target=create.sql
```

Now start the application with the `local` profile active. Spring Boot will create a file called `create.sql` that contains creation scripts for all entities in your application:

```
create table copsboot_user (id uuid not null, email varchar(255), password varchar(255), primary key (id))
create table user_roles (user_id uuid not null, roles varchar(255))
alter table user_roles add constraint FK7je59ku3x462eqxu4ss3das1s foreign key (user_id) references copsboot_user
```

> If your application does not start because there are entities for which there is no database table yet, you can temporarily set `spring.jpa.hibernate.ddl-auto` to `create-drop`. Once you have the `create.sql` file to serve as a basis for your migration file, change `spring.jpa.hibernate.ddl-auto` back to `validate`.

After copying this to your migration file, add a semicolon at the end of each line and some reformatting to end up with this migration file for the users table:

V1.0.0.2__users.sql

```
CREATE TABLE copsboot_user (
  id       UUID NOT NULL,
  email    VARCHAR(255),
  password VARCHAR(255),
  PRIMARY KEY (id)
);

CREATE TABLE user_roles (
  user_id UUID NOT NULL,
  roles   VARCHAR(255)
);

ALTER TABLE user_roles
  ADD CONSTRAINT FK7je59ku3x462eqxu4ss3das1s
FOREIGN KEY (user_id)
REFERENCES copsboot_user;
```

See OAuth Database Schema for the contents of V1.0.0.1__authentication.sql.

To finish, you need to let Spring Boot know which migration scripts to use when. In development, you run with H2, so set spring.flyway.locations accordingly:

application-dev.properties

```
spring.flyway.locations=classpath:db/migration/h2
spring.jpa.hibernate.ddl-auto=create-drop
```

Note that you need to set spring.jpa.hibernate.ddl-auto to create-drop so Hibernate will create the non-auth tables automatically for us.

With the local PostgreSQL, change spring.flyway.locations to use the relevant migrations scripts for that database:

application-local.properties

```
spring.flyway.locations=classpath:db/migration/postgresql
```

Database initialization

Before, you started the application with the dev profile. This triggered Spring Boot to run the DevelopmentDbInitializer bean to create a test user in your system. To get this default test user while using PostgreSQL, you

119

can start up with dev, local as Spring Profiles.

Note that the order is important. You put dev first so that local can overwrite the database properties. With that, you are using your local PostgreSQL database. Since dev is also active, the DevelopmentDbInitializer will run and create your test user.

You only need to start like this once. After that first time, the database will remember the test user so you can start the application with local only.

Updates

Flyway will store a schema_version table in your database so it knows which migrations have already run and which have not. It also stores a checksum of the migration file that was used.

It is very important to *never* update a migration file in your project once you have released this migration to production because Flyway will notice that the checksum no longer matches and will refuse to run anything anymore. This will effectively prevent the startup of your application.

During development, you can just drop all tables and perform the migrations again. But in production, that would be a really bad idea. Once you have released version 1.0 for example, you should not change anything in the migration scripts that already exist. If you want to remove a column or change a column type, you should always create an additional migration file that applies those changes.

Integration testing

H2 is great for testing but it has two major drawbacks:

1. The migrations of PostgreSQL are not run, so they are not tested.
2. H2 is not a perfect replacement for PostgreSQL, so there might be differences in behaviour.

To mitigate these drawbacks, we can use the Testcontainers [https://www.testcontainers.org] project. It uses Docker to start the actual database from a unit test.

To get started, add the dependencies in pom.xml:

Working with a Real Database

```xml
<dependency>
    <groupId>org.testcontainers</groupId>
    <artifactId>testcontainers</artifactId>
    <version>${testcontainers.version}</version>
    <scope>test</scope>
</dependency>
<dependency>
    <groupId>org.testcontainers</groupId>
    <artifactId>postgresql</artifactId>
    <version>${testcontainers.version}</version>
    <scope>test</scope>
</dependency>
```

Use a new Spring Profile integration-test to connect to the Testcontainers-managed PostgreSQL instance. For this, create a new file application-integration-test.properties in the src/test/resources folder:

application-integration-test.properties

```
spring.datasource.url=jdbc:tc:postgresql://localhost/copsbootdb
spring.datasource.driverClassName=org.testcontainers.jdbc.ContainerDatabaseDriver
spring.datasource.username=user
spring.datasource.password=password
spring.jpa.database-platform=org.hibernate.dialect.PostgreSQLDialect
spring.jpa.hibernate.ddl-auto=none

copsboot-security.mobile-app-client-id=test-client-id
copsboot-security.mobile-app-client-secret=test-client-secret

spring.flyway.locations=classpath:db/migration/postgresql
```

Here are some points of interest:

- spring.datasource.url uses the tc prefix. The hostname (localhost) and database name (copsbootdb) don't matter; Testcontainers ignores them.
- spring.datasource.driverClassName uses the Testcontainers JDBC driver. This driver will start a Docker instance with your PostgreSQL database.
- spring.datasource.username is always user and spring.datasource.password is always password.
- spring.jpa.hibernate.ddl-auto is set to none since you want Flyway to create the tables.
- flyway.locations points to the Flyway migrations for PostgreSQL.

Practical Guide to Building an API Back End with Spring Boot

> See JDBC URL [https://www.testcontainers.org/usage/database_containers.html#jdbc-url] for more on different options. For instance, you can choose a specific version like this:
>
> jdbc:tc:mysql:5.6.23://somehostname:someport/databasename

With this in place, you can now create an integration test that will use PostgreSQL:

```
package com.example.copsboot.user;

import com.example.copsboot.infrastructure.SpringProfiles;
import org.junit.Test;
import org.junit.runner.RunWith;
import org.springframework.beans.factory.annotation.Autowired;
import org.springframework.boot.test.autoconfigure.jdbc.AutoConfigureTestDatabase;
import org.springframework.boot.test.autoconfigure.orm.jpa.DataJpaTest;
import org.springframework.jdbc.core.JdbcTemplate;
import org.springframework.test.context.ActiveProfiles;
import org.springframework.test.context.junit4.SpringRunner;

import javax.persistence.EntityManager;
import javax.persistence.PersistenceContext;
import java.util.HashSet;
import java.util.Set;

import static org.assertj.core.api.Assertions.assertThat;

@RunWith(SpringRunner.class)
@DataJpaTest
@AutoConfigureTestDatabase(replace = AutoConfigureTestDatabase.Replace.NONE)
①
@ActiveProfiles(SpringProfiles.INTEGRATION_TEST) ②
public class UserRepositoryIntegrationTest {
    @Autowired
    private UserRepository repository;
    @PersistenceContext
    private EntityManager entityManager;
    @Autowired
    private JdbcTemplate jdbcTemplate;

    @Test
    public void testSaveUser() {
        Set<UserRole> roles = new HashSet<>();
        roles.add(UserRole.OFFICER);
        User user = repository.save(new User(repository.nextId(),
                                              "alex.foley@beverly-hills.com",
```

```
                                "my-secret-pwd",
                                roles));
        assertThat(user).isNotNull();

        assertThat(repository.count()).isEqualTo(1L);

        entityManager.flush(); ③
        assertThat(jdbcTemplate.queryForObject("SELECT count(*) FROM
copsboot_user", Long.class)).isEqualTo(1L); ④
        assertThat(jdbcTemplate.queryForObject("SELECT count(*) FROM
user_roles", Long.class)).isEqualTo(1L);
        assertThat(jdbcTemplate.queryForObject("SELECT roles FROM
user_roles", String.class)).isEqualTo("OFFICER");
    }
}
```

① Configure the testing framework to *not* replace the database with a test database (since you want to use your Testcontainer database).

② Activate the integration-test profile so that the testing framework starts and uses the Testcontainer PostgreSQL database.

③ Make the JPA framework flush all changes to the database so you can inspect the database tables.

④ Run some JDBC queries to validate if the user was properly saved.

Running the test will show output similar to this:

```
2018-07-07 17:25:43 INFO [main] UserRepositoryIntegrationTest - Starting
UserRepositoryIntegrationTest on Wims-MacBook-Pro.local with PID 76847
(started by wdb in /Users/wdb/Projects/spring-boot-book/src/example-
code/chapter07/02 - testcontainers)
2018-07-07 17:25:43 DEBUG [main] UserRepositoryIntegrationTest - Running with
Spring Boot v2.0.3.RELEASE, Spring v5.0.7.RELEASE
2018-07-07 17:25:43 INFO [main] UserRepositoryIntegrationTest - The following
profiles are active: integration-test
2018-07-07 17:25:43 INFO [main] AnnotationConfigApplicationContext -
Refreshing
org.springframework.context.annotation.AnnotationConfigApplicationContext@26d
f6e3a: startup date [Sat Jul 07 17:25:43 CEST 2018]; root of context
hierarchy
2018-07-07 17:25:44 INFO [main] VersionPrinter - Flyway Community Edition
5.0.7 by Boxfuse
            Checking the system...
            Docker version should be at least 1.6.0
            Docker environment should have more than 2GB free disk space
            File should be mountable
2018-07-07 17:26:17 INFO [main] DatabaseFactory - Database:
jdbc:postgresql://localhost:32769/test (PostgreSQL 9.6)
2018-07-07 17:26:18 INFO [main] DbValidate - Successfully validated 2
migrations (execution time 00:00.012s)
2018-07-07 17:26:18 INFO [main] JdbcTableSchemaHistory - Creating Schema
History table: "public"."flyway_schema_history"
2018-07-07 17:26:18 INFO [main] DbMigrate - Current version of schema
"public": << Empty Schema >>
2018-07-07 17:26:18 INFO [main] DbMigrate - Migrating schema "public" to
version 1.0.0.1 - authentication
2018-07-07 17:26:18 INFO [main] DbMigrate - Migrating schema "public" to
version 1.0.0.2 - users
2018-07-07 17:26:18 INFO [main] DbMigrate - Successfully applied 2 migrations
to schema "public" (execution time 00:00.102s)
```

If you would now change something to the migration scripts (e.g., change the email field to email2 in V1.0.0.2__users.sql) and run the test again, you should see it fail, thus proving that you are using the migration scripts you will use in staging and production.

> If you don't want to run these integration tests together with the other unit tests, you will need to configure Maven for that. The easiest way is to have a naming convention (e.g., ending all the integration tests with IntegrationTest) and using the includes/excludes functionality of the Maven Surefire Plugin.

Summary

This chapter has shown how to use a relational database with Spring Boot, and how to ensure that the database is properly initialized by leveraging the Flyway integration in Spring Boot.

Further, you saw how to easily run an integration test against PostgreSQL with Testcontainers.

CHAPTER EIGHT
Validation

An important part of a good API is having proper validation. Nothing is more frustrating than not knowing why the API is not working because everything you try gives a generic *500 Server Error* with no clear indication of the actual problem.

This chapter will show how to apply the standard validators, how to write your own custom validator for a single field or a group of fields on a class, and how to unit-test all that.

Built-in validators

You have already used a few built-in validators in chapter 6 when you implemented a POST call to create a new officer account. To recap, this was the controller method:

```
@PostMapping
@ResponseStatus(HttpStatus.CREATED)
public UserDto createOfficer(@Valid @RequestBody CreateOfficerParameters parameters) {
      User officer = service.createOfficer(parameters.getEmail(),
                                           parameters.getPassword());
      return UserDto.fromUser(officer);
}
```

And this is `CreateOfficerParameters`, which contains the validation annotations:

```
package com.example.copsboot.user.web;

import lombok.Data;
import org.hibernate.validator.constraints.Email;

import javax.validation.constraints.NotNull;
import javax.validation.constraints.Size;

@Data
public class CreateOfficerParameters {
    @NotNull
    @Email
    private String email;

    @NotNull
    @Size(min = 6, max = 1000)
    private String password;
}
```

Validation basically is as simple as adding the @Valid annotation in the controller method and using the validation annotations on the parameter object.

The default validation annotations of the validation API can be found in the javax.validation.constraints package:

- @AssertFalse,
- @AssertTrue,
- @DecimalMax,
- @Digits,
- @Future,
- @Max,
- @Min,
- @NotNull,
- @Null,
- @Past,
- @Pattern, and
- @Size.

Because you have Hibernate Validator on the classpath, you also have access to the following in the org.hibernate.validator.constraints package:

- @CreditCardNumber,
- @EAN,
- @Email,
- @Length,
- @LuhnCheck,
- @Mod10Check,
- @Mod11Check,
- @NotBlank,
- @NotEmpty,
- @Range,
- @SafeHtml, and

- @URL.

Unit test for a built-in validator

You can perform a unit test on this in the `UserRestControllerTest`:

```
@Test
public void testCreateOfficerIfPasswordIsTooShort() throws Exception {
    String email = "wim.deblauwe@example.com";
    String password = "pwd"; ①

    CreateOfficerParameters parameters = new CreateOfficerParameters();
    parameters.setEmail(email);
    parameters.setPassword(password);

    mvc.perform(post("/api/users")
                        .contentType(MediaType.APPLICATION_JSON_UTF8)
.content(objectMapper.writeValueAsString(parameters)))
            .andExpect(status().isBadRequest()) ②
            .andDo(print()); ③

    verify(service, never()).createOfficer(email, password); ④
}
```

① Use a password that is too short to trigger the validation error.

② Check that you get back a *400 Bad Request*.

③ Print the request and response so you can have a look.

④ Ensure the user service is never called. If there is a validation error, no user should be created.

Print the response using the static `MockMvcResultHandlers.print()` method. When running, it will output something like this:

```
Resolved Exception:
             Type =
org.springframework.web.bind.MethodArgumentNotValidException

ModelAndView:
         View name = null
              View = null
             Model = null

FlashMap:
       Attributes = null

MockHttpServletResponse:
            Status = 400
     Error message = null
           Headers = {X-Content-Type-Options=[nosniff], X-XSS-Protection=[1;
mode=block], Cache-Control=[no-cache, no-store, max-age=0, must-revalidate],
Pragma=[no-cache], Expires=[0], X-Frame-Options=[DENY]}
      Content type = null
              Body =
     Forwarded URL = null
     Redirected URL = null
           Cookies = []
```

Note how the body is empty. You have protected your server against invalid input and you notify the client of this fact with the *400 Bad Request* status code. However, it is impolite not to tell your consumer what the problem is.

To do this, implement an exception handler.

Handling validation errors via an exception handler

With Spring Boot, you can react to the validation exception by means of an @ExceptionHandler. Since the exception handler in this case can be reused for all controllers, you can define it in a separate class annotated with @ControllerAdvice:

```
@ControllerAdvice ①
public class RestControllerExceptionHandler {

    @ExceptionHandler ②
    @ResponseBody ③
    @ResponseStatus(HttpStatus.BAD_REQUEST) ④
    public Map<String, List<FieldErrorResponse>>
handle(MethodArgumentNotValidException exception) { ⑤
        return error(exception.getBindingResult()
                              .getFieldErrors()
                              .stream()
                              .map(fieldError -> new
FieldErrorResponse(fieldError.getField(), ⑥

fieldError.getDefaultMessage()))
                              .collect(Collectors.toList()));
    }

    private Map<String, List<FieldErrorResponse>>
error(List<FieldErrorResponse> errors) {
        return Collections.singletonMap("errors", errors);
    }
}
```

① Mark this class as code that will apply to all controllers in the project.

② Mark this method as a method that should be called when an exception is thrown in a controller.

③ This indicates that the return value of the method should be directly used as the response body (after being serialized to JSON).

④ Return this status code when this exception handler is triggered.

⑤ The method name can be anything, but the type of the argument determines the exception to which this method will react. You want to react to `MethodArgumentNotValidException` here. Note that the response output of the unit test above printed this exception class as Resolved Exception.

⑥ Using Java 8 stream operations, create a list of `FieldErrorResponse` objects so that the consumer of your API will receive the name of the field that has a problem and an explanation of what is wrong.

Your exception handler uses the following simple data holder:

Validation

```
@Value
public class FieldErrorResponse {
    private String fieldName;
    private String errorMessage;
}
```

Running the test again results in the following output:

```
MockHttpServletResponse:
           Status = 400
    Error message = null
          Headers = {X-Content-Type-Options=[nosniff], X-XSS-Protection=[1;
mode=block], Cache-Control=[no-cache, no-store, max-age=0, must-revalidate],
Pragma=[no-cache], Expires=[0], X-Frame-Options=[DENY], Content-
Type=[application/json;charset=UTF-8]}
     Content type = application/json;charset=UTF-8
             Body = {"errors":[{"fieldName":"password","errorMessage":"size
must be between 6 and 1000"}]}
    Forwarded URL = null
   Redirected URL = null
          Cookies = []
```

You can now extend the unit test to check the `fieldName` property to ensure that your validation reports the correct fault to your API consumer:

```
    @Test
    public void testCreateOfficerIfPasswordIsTooShort() throws Exception {
        String email = "wim.deblauwe@example.com";
        String password = "pwd";

        CreateOfficerParameters parameters = new CreateOfficerParameters();
        parameters.setEmail(email);
        parameters.setPassword(password);

        mvc.perform(post("/api/users")
                        .contentType(MediaType.APPLICATION_JSON_UTF8)
 .content(objectMapper.writeValueAsString(parameters)))
              .andExpect(status().isBadRequest())
              .andExpect(jsonPath("errors[0].fieldName").value("password")); ①

        verify(service, never()).createOfficer(email, password);
    }
```

① Assert the response body to return the field name that has the validation error.

133

Custom field validator

It is also possible to write your own custom validator. In this chapter, you will create a validator for single field. The next chapter will show how to validate a complete object for when you need to consider multiple fields in the validation.

To make things a bit more interesting, let's extend your application to allow a police officer to post a report to your API. Create the following entity for this:

```
@Entity
public class Report extends AbstractEntity<ReportId> {
    @ManyToOne
    private User reporter;
    private ZonedDateTime dateTime;
    private String description;

    @ArtifactForFramework
    protected Report() {
    }

    public Report(ReportId id, User reporter, ZonedDateTime dateTime, String description) {
        super(id);
        this.reporter = reporter;
        this.dateTime = dateTime;
        this.description = description;
    }

    public User getReporter() {
        return reporter;
    }

    public ZonedDateTime getDateTime() {
        return dateTime;
    }

    public String getDescription() {
        return description;
    }
}
```

Now create the following classes/interfaces according to the same principles you used when creating the User entity counterparts:

- ReportId,

Validation

- ReportRepository,
- ReportRepositoryCustom,
- ReportRepositoryImpl,
- ReportService, and
- ReportServiceImpl.

Finally, in a web subpackage, create the ReportRestController:

```
@RestController
@RequestMapping("/api/reports")
public class ReportRestController {
    private final ReportService service;

    public ReportRestController(ReportService service) {
        this.service = service;
    }

    @PostMapping
    @ResponseStatus(HttpStatus.CREATED)
    public ReportDto createReport(@AuthenticationPrincipal ApplicationUserDetails userDetails,
                                  @Valid @RequestBody CreateReportParameters parameters) {
        return ReportDto.fromReport(service.createReport(userDetails.getUserId(),
                                    parameters.getDateTime(),
                                    parameters.getDescription()));
    }
}
```

This has the following parameter object:

```
@Data
@AllArgsConstructor
@NoArgsConstructor
public class CreateReportParameters {
    private ZonedDateTime dateTime;
    private String description;
}
```

The POST returns a JSON response modelled by the ReportDto class:

```
@Value
public class ReportDto {
    private ReportId id;
    private String reporter;
    private ZonedDateTime dateTime;
    private String description;

    public static ReportDto fromReport(Report report) {
        return new ReportDto(report.getId(),
                             report.getReporter().getEmail(),
                             report.getDateTime(),
                             report.getDescription());
    }
}
```

This is the accompanying unit test that will show that the basic flow works:

```java
@RunWith(SpringRunner.class)
@CopsbootControllerTest(ReportRestController.class)
public class ReportRestControllerTest {
    @Autowired
    private MockMvc mvc;

    @Autowired
    private ObjectMapper objectMapper;
    @MockBean
    private ReportService service;

    @Test
    public void officerIsAbleToPostAReport() throws Exception {
        String accessToken = obtainAccessToken(mvc, Users.OFFICER_EMAIL, Users.OFFICER_PASSWORD);
        ZonedDateTime dateTime = ZonedDateTime.parse("2018-04-11T22:59:03.189+02:00");
        String description = "This is a test report description.";
        CreateReportParameters parameters = new CreateReportParameters(dateTime, description);
        when(service.createReport(eq(Users.officer().getId()), any(ZonedDateTime.class), eq(description)))
                .thenReturn(new Report(new ReportId(UUID.randomUUID()), Users.officer(), dateTime, description));

        mvc.perform(post("/api/reports")
                            .header(HEADER_AUTHORIZATION, bearer(accessToken))
                            .contentType(MediaType.APPLICATION_JSON_UTF8)
                            .content(objectMapper.writeValueAsString(parameters)))
           .andExpect(status().isCreated())
           .andExpect(jsonPath("id").exists())
           .andExpect(jsonPath("reporter").value(Users.OFFICER_EMAIL))
           .andExpect(jsonPath("dateTime").value("2018-04-11T22:59:03.189+02:00"))
           .andExpect(jsonPath("description").value(description));
    }
}
```

To show how to create a custom validator, let's create a check of whether or not the police officer described a suspect in the submitted report. To do this, you will simply check if the word suspect appears in the report's description field.

The first thing you need to do is to create an annotation that you can then add to the description field. For this example, call it

@ValidReportDescription:

```
package com.example.copsboot.report.web;

import javax.validation.Constraint;
import javax.validation.Payload;
import java.lang.annotation.ElementType;
import java.lang.annotation.Retention;
import java.lang.annotation.RetentionPolicy;
import java.lang.annotation.Target;

@Target(ElementType.FIELD) ①
@Retention(RetentionPolicy.RUNTIME) ②
@Constraint(validatedBy = {ReportDescriptionValidator.class}) ③
public @interface ValidReportDescription {
    String message() default "Invalid report description"; ④

    Class<?>[] groups() default {}; ⑤

    Class<? extends Payload>[] payload() default {}; ⑥
}
```

① Your annotation can be applied to a field of a class.

② The annotation must be available at run time.

③ The `ReportDescriptionValidator` class will contain your custom validation logic and will validate the field.

④ This is the default message if validation fails.

⑤ Allows to specify validation groups for our constraints

⑥ Can be used by clients of the Bean Validation API to assign custom payload objects to a constraint

`ReportDescriptionValidator` validates the `@ValidReportDescription` annotation:

Validation

```
package com.example.copsboot.report.web;

import javax.validation.ConstraintValidator;
import javax.validation.ConstraintValidatorContext;

public class ReportDescriptionValidator implements
ConstraintValidator<ValidReportDescription, String> { ①

    @Override
    public void initialize(ValidReportDescription constraintAnnotation) { ②
    }

    @Override
    public boolean isValid(String value, ConstraintValidatorContext context)
{
        boolean result = true;
        if (!value.toLowerCase().contains("suspect")) { ③
            result = false;
        }
        return result;
    }
}
```

① A validator must implement the ConstraintValidator interface with two generic types. The first one is the used annotation. The second is the type that the annotation can be attached to.

② The initialize method allows you to take information from the annotation to parameterize the validation process.

③ Do the actual validation logic and return false if the validation fails.

The final step is using the annotation on your CreateReportParameters class:

```
@Data
@AllArgsConstructor
@NoArgsConstructor
public class CreateReportParameters {
    private ZonedDateTime dateTime;

    @ValidReportDescription
    private String description;
}
```

To ensure that everything is working, write the following unit test:

ReportDescriptionValidatorTest.java

```
    @Test
    public void givenEmptyString_notValid() {
        ValidatorFactory factory = Validation.buildDefaultValidatorFactory();
①
        Validator validator = factory.getValidator(); ②

        CreateReportParameters parameters = new
CreateReportParameters(ZonedDateTime.now(), "");
        Set<ConstraintViolation<CreateReportParameters>> violationSet =
validator.validate(parameters); ③
        assertThat(violationSet).hasViolationOnPath("description"); ④
    }
```

① Get the default `ValidatorFactory`.

② Ask for the `Validator`.

③ Using the `Validator`, validate the object.

④ Assert that there is a validation error on the `description` field.

You should of course also test the valid case:

ReportDescriptionValidatorTest.java

```
    @Test
    public void givenSuspectWordPresent_valid() {
        ValidatorFactory factory = Validation.buildDefaultValidatorFactory();
        Validator validator = factory.getValidator();

        CreateReportParameters parameters = new
CreateReportParameters(ZonedDateTime.now(),
                                                                     "The
suspect was wearing a black hat.");
        Set<ConstraintViolation<CreateReportParameters>> violationSet =
validator.validate(parameters);
        assertThat(violationSet).hasNoViolations();
    }
```

> The assert statement uses a custom AssertJ assertion. See my blog [https://wimdeblauwe.wordpress.com/2017/01/22/assertj-custom-assertion-for-constraintvalidator-tests/] for how that works.

Custom object validator

You can also validate a whole object instead of a single field. To do this, add two new properties to report creation: `trafficIncident` and `numberOfInvolvedCars`. The logic will be that if `trafficIncident` is `true` then `numberOfInvolvedCars` is supposed to be 1 or more.

First, adjust `CreateReportsParameters`:

```
@Data
@AllArgsConstructor
@NoArgsConstructor
@ValidCreateReportParameters
public class CreateReportParameters {
    private ZonedDateTime dateTime;

    @ValidReportDescription
    private String description;

    private boolean trafficIncident;
    private int numberOfInvolvedCars;
}
```

Note that your new annotation `@ValidCreateReportParameters` has been added as a class-level annotation. This is the code you need for it:

```
@Target(ElementType.TYPE) ①
@Retention(RetentionPolicy.RUNTIME)
@Constraint(validatedBy = {CreateReportParametersValidator.class}) ②
public @interface ValidCreateReportParameters {
    String message() default "Invalid report";

    Class<?>[] groups() default {};

    Class<? extends Payload>[] payload() default {};
```

① Indicate this annotation should be added to the class.

② The validator to use is `CreateReportParametersValidator`.

Finally, here is the validator itself:

```
public class CreateReportParametersValidator implements
ConstraintValidator<ValidCreateReportParameters, CreateReportParameters> { ①

    @Override
    public void initialize(ValidCreateReportParameters constraintAnnotation)
{
    }

    @Override
    public boolean isValid(CreateReportParameters value,
ConstraintValidatorContext context) {
        boolean result = true;
        if (value.isTrafficIncident() && value.getNumberOfInvolvedCars() <=
0) { ②
            result = false;
        }
        return result;
    }
```

① Use the correct generic types for the used annotation and class that is annotated.

② Do the correct test and return false when the combination of parameters is invalid.

Next up, write a test to validate your validation logic.

If trafficIncident is true and numberOfInvolvedCars is 0, then you should get a violation on the root path (indicated with the empty string):

```
@Test
public void givenTrafficIndicentButInvolvedCarsZero_invalid() {
    ValidatorFactory factory = Validation.buildDefaultValidatorFactory();
    Validator validator = factory.getValidator();

    CreateReportParameters parameters = new
CreateReportParameters(ZonedDateTime.now(),
                                                                   "The
suspect was wearing a black hat",
                                                                   true,
                                                                   0);
    Set<ConstraintViolation<CreateReportParameters>> violationSet =
validator.validate(parameters);
    assertThat(violationSet).hasViolationOnPath("");
}
```

If trafficIncident is true and numberOfInvolvedCars is 2, then there is no violation:

```
@Test
public void givenTrafficIndicent_involvedCarsMustBePositive() {
    ValidatorFactory factory = Validation.buildDefaultValidatorFactory();
    Validator validator = factory.getValidator();

    CreateReportParameters parameters = new CreateReportParameters(ZonedDateTime.now(),
                                                                    "The suspect was wearing a black hat.",
                                                                    true,
                                                                    2);
    Set<ConstraintViolation<CreateReportParameters>> violationSet = validator.validate(parameters);
    assertThat(violationSet).hasNoViolations();
}
```

If `trafficIncident` is false, then there is also no violation:

```
@Test
public void givenNoTrafficIndicent_involvedCarsDoesNotMatter() {
    ValidatorFactory factory = Validation.buildDefaultValidatorFactory();
    Validator validator = factory.getValidator();

    CreateReportParameters parameters = new CreateReportParameters(ZonedDateTime.now(),
                                                                    "The suspect was wearing a black hat.",
                                                                    false,
                                                                    0);
    Set<ConstraintViolation<CreateReportParameters>> violationSet = validator.validate(parameters);
    assertThat(violationSet).hasNoViolations();
}
```

Custom object validator using a Spring service

ReportDescriptionValidator and CreateReportParametersValidator are fairly simple as they do not need any other class to perform the validation. But what if, when creating a new user, you need to validate that there is no existing user in the database with the new user's requested email address?

Your validator will need a reference to the UserService to check this. Luckily, this is easy using Spring Boot.

To get started, create a new annotation @ValidCreateUserParameters:

```
@Target(ElementType.TYPE) ①
@Retention(RetentionPolicy.RUNTIME)
@Constraint(validatedBy = {CreateUserParametersValidator.class}) ②
public @interface ValidCreateUserParameters {
    String message() default "Invalid user";

    Class<?>[] groups() default {};

    Class<? extends Payload>[] payload() default {};
}
```

① This is a class-level annotation, so use ElementType.TYPE.

② Validation will be handled by CreateUserParametersValidator.

Next, create your actual validator:

```
public class CreateUserParametersValidator implements
ConstraintValidator<ValidCreateUserParameters, CreateOfficerParameters> {

    private final UserService userService;

    @Autowired
    public CreateUserParametersValidator(UserService userService) { ①
        this.userService = userService;
    }

    @Override
    public void initialize(ValidCreateUserParameters constraintAnnotation) {

    }

    @Override
    public boolean isValid(CreateOfficerParameters userParameters,
ConstraintValidatorContext context) {

        boolean result = true;

        if
(userService.findUserByEmail(userParameters.getEmail()).isPresent()) { ②
            context.buildConstraintViolationWithTemplate(
                    "There is already a user with the given email address.")
                    .addPropertyNode("email").addConstraintViolation(); ③

            result = false; ④
        }

        return result;
    }
}
```

① Autowire the UserService so you can ask it if there already is a user with the given email address.

② Check for the presence of a user.

③ If so, update the context object with the error.

④ Return false to indicate that the validation has failed.

And that is all there is to it. To prove it all works, create the following test:

```
@RunWith(SpringRunner.class)
@SpringBootTest  ①
@ActiveProfiles(SpringProfiles.TEST)
public class CreateUserParametersValidatorTest {

    @MockBean
    private UserService userService;  ②
    @Autowired
    private PasswordEncoder encoder;
    @Autowired
    private ValidatorFactory factory;  ③

    @Test
    public void invalidIfAlreadyUserWithGivenEmail() {

        String email = "wim.deblauwe@example.com";
        when(userService.findUserByEmail(email))
                .thenReturn(Optional.of(
                        User.createOfficer(new UserId(UUID.randomUUID()),
                                            email,
                                            encoder.encode("testing1234"))));

        Validator validator = factory.getValidator();  ④

        CreateOfficerParameters userParameters = new
CreateOfficerParameters();
        userParameters.setEmail(email);
        userParameters.setPassword("my-secret-pwd-1234");
        Set<ConstraintViolation<CreateOfficerParameters>> violationSet =
validator.validate(userParameters);  ⑤
        assertThat(violationSet).hasViolationSize(2)
                                .hasViolationOnPath("email");  ⑥
    }

    @Test
    public void validIfNoUserWithGivenEmail() {
        String email = "wim.deblauwe@example.com";
        when(userService.findUserByEmail(email))
                .thenReturn(Optional.empty());

        Validator validator = factory.getValidator();

        CreateOfficerParameters userParameters = new
CreateOfficerParameters();
        userParameters.setEmail(email);
        userParameters.setPassword("my-secret-pwd-1234");
        Set<ConstraintViolation<CreateOfficerParameters>> violationSet =
validator.validate(userParameters);
        assertThat(violationSet).hasNoViolations();
    }
}
```

① Start the full application context in the test.
② Create a mock UserService so you can tell it how to behave.
③ Autowire the ValidatorFactory so you can do your validation test.
④ Get the actual Validator from the factory.
⑤ Validate the CreateOfficerParameters object.
⑥ Check if there is indeed a validator error on the email path.

> There are two validation errors in violationSet because the object itself is invalid (since your annotation applies to the object) and you have manually added a violation on the email field in your validator.

Summary

You have seen how to use validators and how to implement your own custom validation. You have written unit tests to ensure the validators are correct.

In the next chapter, you will learn about uploading files.

CHAPTER NINE

File Upload

Many APIs need to support file uploads. In many cases, these are images but could be any kind of file. This chapter will show how to support this, and give some pointers on how to validate the incoming file.

Upload a file

As an example, you will allow the user of your API to add an image when creating a new report. The first thing you must do is to add an extra field to CreateReportParameters:

```
@Data
@AllArgsConstructor
@NoArgsConstructor
public class CreateReportParameters {
    @DateTimeFormat(iso = DateTimeFormat.ISO.DATE_TIME)
    private ZonedDateTime dateTime;

    @ValidReportDescription
    private String description;

    @NotNull
    private MultipartFile image;  ①
}
```

① This is the image field of type org.springframework.web.multipart.MultipartFile.

Next, update the method signature of your controller. This is what you had:

com.example.copsboot.report.web.ReportRestController

```
    @PostMapping
    @ResponseStatus(HttpStatus.CREATED)
    public ReportDto createReport(@AuthenticationPrincipal
ApplicationUserDetails userDetails,
                                  @Valid @RequestBody CreateReportParameters
parameters) {
```

Because you now want to allow files to be uploaded, you can no longer use a JSON body. By removing @RequestBody, the method will permit the use of multipart/form-data instead:

com.example.copsboot.report.web.ReportRestController

```
@PostMapping
@ResponseStatus(HttpStatus.CREATED)
public ReportDto createReport(@AuthenticationPrincipal
   ApplicationUserDetails userDetails,
                              @Valid CreateReportParameters parameters) {
```

To ensure that this all works properly, update `ReportRestControllerTest` to validate it:

```java
@RunWith(SpringRunner.class)
@CopsbootControllerTest(ReportRestController.class)
public class ReportRestControllerTest {
    @Autowired
    private MockMvc mvc;

    @MockBean
    private ReportService service;

    @Test
    public void officerIsAbleToPostAReport() throws Exception {
        String accessToken = obtainAccessToken(mvc, Users.OFFICER_EMAIL,
Users.OFFICER_PASSWORD);
        String dateTime = "2018-04-11T22:59:03.189+02:00";
        String description = "The suspect is wearing a black hat.";
        MockMultipartFile image = createMockImage();
        when(service.createReport(eq(Users.officer().getId()),
                                  any(ZonedDateTime.class),
                                  eq(description),
                                  any(MockMultipartFile.class)))
                .thenReturn(new Report(new ReportId(UUID.randomUUID()),
Users.officer(), ZonedDateTime.parse(dateTime), description));

        mvc.perform(fileUpload("/api/reports")  ①
                            .file(image)  ②
                            .header(HEADER_AUTHORIZATION,
bearer(accessToken))
                            .param("dateTime", dateTime)  ③
                            .param("description", description))
            .andExpect(status().isCreated())
            .andExpect(jsonPath("id").exists())
            .andExpect(jsonPath("reporter").value(Users.OFFICER_EMAIL))
            .andExpect(jsonPath("dateTime").value(dateTime))
            .andExpect(jsonPath("description").value(description));
    }

    private MockMultipartFile createMockImage() {  ④
        return new MockMultipartFile("image",
                                     "picture.png",
                                     "image/png",
                                     new byte[]{1, 2, 3});
    }
}
```

① Use `MockMvcRequestBuilders.fileUpload()` to simulate uploading a file.

② Specify the `MultipartFile` via the `file()` method.

③ Other fields from the `CreateReportParameters` object are added via the `param()` method.

④ Use `MockMultipartFile` from Spring Test for your testing. Note that it is important that the first argument ("image") of the constructor matches the field name in `CreateReportParameters`.

File-size validation

One common task is ensuring that the file size does not exceed a certain limit to protect your server. Spring Boot lets you easily configure this. Just add the following lines to application.properties:

```
spring.servlet.multipart.max-file-size=1MB
spring.servlet.multipart.max-request-size=10MB
```

- `spring.servlet.multipart.max-file-size` specifies the maximum size per file in megabytes (MB), kilobytes (KB), or bytes (no suffix).
- `spring.servlet.multipart.max-request-size` specifies the maximum size for the whole multipart request.

You can no longer use `MockMvc` to test this. As Tomcat, not Spring Boot itself, handles this, you need to set up an integration test with an embedded Tomcat for testing. Instead of `MockMvc`, use the REST Assured [http://rest-assured.io/] library.

First, add the dependency to your Maven pom.xml:

```xml
<dependency>
    <groupId>io.rest-assured</groupId>
    <artifactId>rest-assured</artifactId>
    <version>${rest-assured.version}</version>
    <scope>test</scope>
</dependency>
```

Set the version to 3.1.0, the most recent version at the time of writing:

```xml
<properties>
  ...
  <rest-assured.version>3.1.0</rest-assured.version>
</properties>
```

You can now create your integration test:

```java
@RunWith(SpringRunner.class)
@SpringBootTest(webEnvironment = SpringBootTest.WebEnvironment.RANDOM_PORT)
①
@ActiveProfiles(SpringProfiles.TEST)
public class ReportRestControllerIntegrationTest {

    @LocalServerPort
    private int serverport; ②

    @Autowired
    private UserService userService;

    @Before
    public void setup() {
        RestAssured.port = serverport; ③
        RestAssured.enableLoggingOfRequestAndResponseIfValidationFails(); ④
    }

    @Test
    public void officerIsUnableToPostAReportIfFileSizeIsTooBig() {

        userService.createOfficer(Users.OFFICER_EMAIL, Users.OFFICER_PASSWORD); ⑤

        String dateTime = "2018-04-11T22:59:03.189+02:00";
        String description = "The suspect is wearing a black hat.";

        SecurityHelperForRestAssured.givenAuthenticatedUser(serverport, Users.OFFICER_EMAIL, Users.OFFICER_PASSWORD) ⑥
                .when()
                .multiPart("image", new MultiPartSpecBuilder(new byte[2_000_000]) ⑦
                        .fileName("picture.png")
                        .mimeType("image/png")
                        .build())
                .formParam("dateTime", dateTime)
                .formParam("description", description)
                .post("/api/reports")
                .then()
   .statusCode(HttpStatus.BAD_REQUEST.value())); ⑧
    }
}
```

① Set the `webEnvironment` to a random free port so that the embedded Tomcat is started.

② Inject the random port into the `serverport` field via the `@LocalServerPort` annotation.

③ Configure REST Assured to use the random port for doing the calls.

File Upload

④ Configure REST Assured to log requests and responses when validation fails so you can see what is going on.

⑤ Create your test user.

⑥ Get an authentication token for doing the call using SecurityHelperForRestAssured (see below).

⑦ Specify the file size via the byte array to be larger than that allowed in your spring.http.multipart.max-file-size setting.

⑧ Validate that you get a *400 Bad Request* back.

However, when you run this, you don't get the *400 Bad Request* but instead get a *500 Internal Server Error*:

```
{
    "timestamp": "2018-04-24T15:23:06.516+0000",
    "status": 500,
    "error": "Internal Server Error",
    "exception": "org.springframework.web.multipart.MultipartException",
    "message": "Could not parse multipart servlet request; nested exception
is java.lang.IllegalStateException:
org.apache.tomcat.util.http.fileupload.FileUploadBase$FileSizeLimitExceededEx
ception: The field image exceeds its maximum permitted size of 1048576
bytes.",
    "path": "/api/reports"
}
```

Before learning how to fix this, look at SecurityHelperForRestAssured:

155

```java
package com.example.copsboot.infrastructure.security;

import io.restassured.specification.RequestSpecification;
import org.springframework.security.oauth2.client.OAuth2RestTemplate;
import org.springframework.security.oauth2.client.token.grant.password.ResourceOwnerPasswordResourceDetails;
import org.springframework.security.oauth2.common.OAuth2AccessToken;

import static io.restassured.RestAssured.given;
import static java.lang.String.format;

public class SecurityHelperForRestAssured {
    private static final String UNIT_TEST_CLIENT_ID = "test-client-id"; ①
    private static final String UNIT_TEST_CLIENT_SECRET = "test-client-secret"; ②

    public static RequestSpecification givenAuthenticatedUser(int serverPort, String username, String password) {
        OAuth2RestTemplate template = new OAuth2RestTemplate(createResourceOwnerPasswordResourceDetails(serverPort,
                                                                                                        username,
                                                                                                        password));
        OAuth2AccessToken accessToken = template.getAccessToken();

        return given().auth().preemptive().oauth2(accessToken.getValue());
    }

    private static ResourceOwnerPasswordResourceDetails createResourceOwnerPasswordResourceDetails(int serverPort, String username, String password) {
        ResourceOwnerPasswordResourceDetails details = new ResourceOwnerPasswordResourceDetails();

        details.setAccessTokenUri(String.format("http://localhost:%s/oauth/token", serverPort));
        details.setUsername(username);
        details.setPassword(password);
        details.setClientId(UNIT_TEST_CLIENT_ID);
        details.setClientSecret(UNIT_TEST_CLIENT_SECRET);
        return details;
    }
}
```

① This needs to match what you specify in `application-test.properties`.

② This needs to match what you specify in `application-test.properties`.

As you can see, you get the OAuth2 access token for the given user/password combination and use that one for the actual call that the unit/integration test wants to do.

To fix your test so that the controller returns a *400 Bad Request*, you need to update `RestControllerExceptionHandler`. In the JSON response in your test, you see that you get an exception of type `org.springframework.web.multipart.MultipartException`. If you now add a method that catches that exception and turns it into a proper response code, your unit test will pass.

com.example.copsboot.infrastructure.mvc.RestControllerExceptionHandler

```
@ExceptionHandler(MultipartException.class)
public ResponseEntity handleMultipartException(MultipartException e,
Model model) {
    model.addAttribute("exception", e);
    return ResponseEntity
            .badRequest()
            .body(e.getMessage());
}
```

If you now run the test again, all will be green.

Summary

This chapter has shown how to implement file upload for your API and how to set a maximum file size.

Action!

I hope you have learned a lot from this book and I am looking forward to seeing more great applications using the amazing Spring Boot framework.

Additional reading

If you want to learn more, here are some suggestions:

- Spring Boot Reference Guide [https://docs.spring.io/spring-boot/docs/2.0.3.RELEASE/reference/htmlsingle/] — Phillip Webb, Dave Syer, Josh Long, Stéphane Nicoll, Rob Winch, Andy Wilkinson, Marcel Overdijk, Christian Dupuis, Sébastien Deleuze, Michael Simons, Vedran Pavić, Jay Bryant, Madhura Bhave

- *Learning Spring Boot 2.0* [https://www.packtpub.com/application-development/learning-spring-boot-20-second-edition] — Greg L. Turnquist (Packt Publishing, 2017)

- *Spring in Action* (Fifth edition) [https://www.manning.com/books/spring-in-action-fifth-edition] — Craig Walls (Manning, expected 2018)

- Spring Tips [https://www.youtube.com/playlist?list=PLgGXSWYM2FpPw8rV0tZoMiJYSCiLhPnOc] — YouTube playlist

- *Spring Boot in Action* [https://www.manning.com/books/spring-boot-in-action] — Craig Walls (Manning, 2015)

> *Spring Boot in Action* covers Spring Boot 1.x.

About the Author

Wim Deblauwe is a software engineer who has been working mainly with Java for the past 20 years. He has developed and designed various IoT-related projects that have seen deployments worldwide. He also works with JavaScript, Python, PHP, and ActionScript if the project calls for it.

In the last three years, he has worked for PegusApps, a Belgium-based remote-first company that focuses on being an innovation partner to other companies for software development. Implementing various challenging projects with Spring Boot and mobile applications at PegusApps has really accelerated his learning.

If Deblauwe is not programming, he is playing the guitar, writing songs, or enjoying a good meal.

Appendix A: OAuth Database Schema

This contains the scripts for creating various databases for the OAuth tables.

PostgreSQL

```sql
CREATE TABLE oauth_client_details (
  client_id               VARCHAR(256) PRIMARY KEY,
  resource_ids            VARCHAR(256),
  client_secret           VARCHAR(256),
  scope                   VARCHAR(256),
  authorized_grant_types  VARCHAR(256),
  web_server_redirect_uri VARCHAR(256),
  authorities             VARCHAR(256),
  access_token_validity   INTEGER,
  refresh_token_validity  INTEGER,
  additional_information  VARCHAR(4096),
  autoapprove             VARCHAR(256)
);

CREATE TABLE oauth_client_token (
  token_id          VARCHAR(256),
  token             BYTEA,
  authentication_id VARCHAR(256) PRIMARY KEY,
  user_name         VARCHAR(256),
  client_id         VARCHAR(256)
);

CREATE TABLE oauth_access_token (
  token_id          VARCHAR(256),
  token             BYTEA,
  authentication_id VARCHAR(256) PRIMARY KEY,
  user_name         VARCHAR(256),
  client_id         VARCHAR(256),
  authentication    BYTEA,
  refresh_token     VARCHAR(256)
);

CREATE TABLE oauth_refresh_token (
  token_id       VARCHAR(256),
  token          BYTEA,
  authentication BYTEA
);

CREATE TABLE oauth_code (
  code           VARCHAR(256),
  authentication BYTEA
);

CREATE TABLE oauth_approvals (
  userId         VARCHAR(256),
  clientId       VARCHAR(256),
  scope          VARCHAR(256),
  status         VARCHAR(10),
  expiresAt      TIMESTAMP,
  lastModifiedAt TIMESTAMP
);
```

Appendix A: OAuth Database Schema

MySQL

```
CREATE TABLE oauth_client_details (
  client_id               VARCHAR(255) PRIMARY KEY,
  resource_ids            VARCHAR(255),
  client_secret           VARCHAR(255),
  scope                   VARCHAR(255),
  authorized_grant_types  VARCHAR(255),
  web_server_redirect_uri VARCHAR(255),
  authorities             VARCHAR(255),
  access_token_validity   INTEGER,
  refresh_token_validity  INTEGER,
  additional_information  VARCHAR(4096),
  autoapprove             TINYINT
);

CREATE TABLE oauth_client_token (
  token_id          VARCHAR(255),
  token             BLOB,
  authentication_id VARCHAR(255) PRIMARY KEY,
  user_name         VARCHAR(255),
  client_id         VARCHAR(255)
);

CREATE TABLE oauth_access_token (
  token_id          VARCHAR(255),
  token             BLOB,
  authentication_id VARCHAR(255) PRIMARY KEY,
  user_name         VARCHAR(255),
  client_id         VARCHAR(255),
  authentication    BLOB,
  refresh_token     VARCHAR(255)
);

CREATE TABLE oauth_refresh_token (
  token_id       VARCHAR(255),
  token          BLOB,
  authentication BLOB
);

CREATE TABLE oauth_code (
  activationCode VARCHAR(255),
  authentication BLOB
);
```

Microsoft SQL Server

```
CREATE TABLE oauth_client_details (
  client_id               VARCHAR(255) PRIMARY KEY,
  resource_ids            VARCHAR(255),
  client_secret           VARCHAR(255),
  scope                   VARCHAR(255),
  authorized_grant_types  VARCHAR(255),
  web_server_redirect_uri VARCHAR(255),
  authorities             VARCHAR(255),
  access_token_validity   INTEGER,
  refresh_token_validity  INTEGER,
  additional_information  VARCHAR(4096),
  autoapprove             TINYINT
);

CREATE TABLE oauth_client_token (
  token_id          VARCHAR(255),
  token             VARBINARY(max),
  authentication_id VARCHAR(255) PRIMARY KEY,
  user_name         VARCHAR(255),
  client_id         VARCHAR(255)
);

CREATE TABLE oauth_access_token (
  token_id          VARCHAR(255),
  token             VARBINARY(max),
  authentication_id VARCHAR(255) PRIMARY KEY,
  user_name         VARCHAR(255),
  client_id         VARCHAR(255),
  authentication    VARBINARY(max),
  refresh_token     VARCHAR(255)
);

CREATE TABLE oauth_refresh_token (
  token_id       VARCHAR(255),
  token          VARBINARY(max),
  authentication VARBINARY(max)
);

CREATE TABLE oauth_code (
  activationCode VARCHAR(255),
  authentication VARBINARY(max)
);
```

H2

Appendix A: OAuth Database Schema

```sql
CREATE TABLE oauth_client_details (
  client_id               VARCHAR(255) PRIMARY KEY,
  resource_ids            VARCHAR(255),
  client_secret           VARCHAR(255),
  scope                   VARCHAR(255),
  authorized_grant_types  VARCHAR(255),
  web_server_redirect_uri VARCHAR(255),
  authorities             VARCHAR(255),
  access_token_validity   INTEGER,
  refresh_token_validity  INTEGER,
  additional_information  VARCHAR(4096),
  autoapprove             VARCHAR(255)
);

CREATE TABLE oauth_client_token (
  token_id          VARCHAR(255),
  token             BLOB,
  authentication_id VARCHAR(255) PRIMARY KEY,
  user_name         VARCHAR(255),
  client_id         VARCHAR(255)
);

CREATE TABLE oauth_access_token (
  token_id          VARCHAR(255),
  token             BLOB,
  authentication_id VARCHAR(255) PRIMARY KEY,
  user_name         VARCHAR(255),
  client_id         VARCHAR(255),
  authentication    BLOB,
  refresh_token     VARCHAR(255)
);

CREATE TABLE oauth_refresh_token (
  token_id       VARCHAR(255),
  token          BLOB,
  authentication BLOB
);

CREATE TABLE oauth_code (
  activationCode VARCHAR(255),
  authentication BLOB
);
```

Printed in Great Britain
by Amazon